HELP!

I'm a
Sunday
School
Teacher

HELP!

I'm a Sunday School Teacher

Mary Duckert

PRESBYTERIAN
PUBLISHING
CORPORATION

Presbyterian Publishing Corporation
Louisville, Kentucky

Book design by Diane Bridgwater Cooke
Illustrations by Debora Weber

Revised edition

PRINTED IN THE UNITED STATES OF AMERICA

ISBN 1–57153–201–3

To Mabel Hoveland Duckert, who taught me
without knowing how at Bryn Mawr Church,
Cottage Grove, Wisconsin

Contents

CHAPTER 3

CHAPTER 4

CHAPTER 5

WELCOME!

So you've been asked to teach church school. Welcome to the club! You'll soon find out that we are a peculiar lot. We span the range from teenagers to keenagers. Some of us play the guitar and lead singing, while a few of us couldn't carry a tune in a bucket. Some of us are artists and others of us end up gluing the crayons together.

A great many of us have taught for only a year or two and don't intend to teach forever. We've received training and encouragement, and we're beginning to feel that we aren't wasting our time or, worse yet, wasting the time of those we teach. Some of us are particularly adept with children. A few of us are helping two-year-olds tolerate an hour or two away from their families, helping them learn how to survive, surrounded by walking, talking human beings exactly the same size as they are.

We know how to do countless things when we begin adding up the talents. We compute income tax for people, drive school buses, anchor the evening TV news, direct day care centers for children, teach adults newly arrived in our midst to converse in our language, sell real estate, check out groceries, sing golden oldies with Alzheimer's patients. The list is almost endless.

But we have one thing in common, which is what makes us the club we are. We all had a first day and a first year. With the exception of the day school teachers, few of us felt we were prepared to teach. Some of us thought we could do the job sitting on our hands, but most of us were not at all sure what we would do faced for the first time with a group of children or young people who expected something from us.

We all found out it is not easy to teach. Even some of the day school teachers discovered their limitations when confronted with less than one hour a week, a new subject, sporadic attendance, and a volunteer administration running the school. It is probably close to folly to expect that anything significant can happen in the life of a child who attends church school on one day a week taught by willing volunteers. It is probably an inefficient way to educate, but this is the system most of us have.

Slowly our methods, curriculum materials, physical plants, and education of teachers have improved our time with children. Some of us remember the days when hundreds of boys and girls thronged to two and three sessions of instruction in newly built educational facilities outgrown before the sawdust was swept from the floors. It is tempting to look with nostalgia at those times when education in the faith was a high-priority item, financing full-time specialists in local churches, regions, and denominational offices. But those of us who were there and are also in the here and now spend little time in self-congratulation. Curriculum materials have never taught themselves. And teacher training events do not educate the people who choose to be absent.

The job of your church is the same as it was in its so-called Golden Age: to prepare you to be a competent teacher. It is your responsibility to accept the efforts of the church and do the best you can.

There is one aspect of church school teaching that is peculiar to church education. We are not expected to *make* Christians of the persons we teach. Salvation is God's work. The Bible is clear about that. Whenever teachers put that burden on themselves, they fail. Our work is to open the Scriptures, excite curiosity, support thoughtful inquiry, and be around when important decisions are being made.

When we take time to reflect, we remember, when we sit back and rock for a while, that religious education goes on outside our classrooms too. We can teach five- and six-year-olds that God loves them and knows them by name. But when they are told by well-meaning caregivers at the drive-by shooting of a schoolmate that God "took him away to heaven," why should they believe that God will favor them in their daily lives? Older children and young people can paint a "faith"-ful family tree, going back to Abraham and Sarah with their own branches reaching into the twenty-first century. With the church's blessing they can share a Seder meal at Passover with Jewish families and invite their friends from the synagogue to a celebration of Pentecost. But how can we help them understand the motivations of their neighbors who spray-paint "Jew Lovers" on the church building and attempt to burn the synagogue?

Constructive religious education outside the classroom happens too. That is why our job must be done well. We teach that a neighbor is anyone, anywhere, who needs our help. Suddenly those who learned that concept find themselves helpless except for the help from others they have never met. We teach that God is with us in life and in death. How much more about this mystery a person learns when someone close to him or her is bolstered by this belief at a time of sorrow.

We teach that God the Creator forgives and that God's children repent—turn around and set things straight. But only after the whole church community demonstrates pardon for the "unforgivable" to one of God's children can we be sure we are seriously teaching anything about grace. There would be little hope for our teaching the Christian's responsibility to the neighbor, the presence of God, and forgiveness if we could not count on steadfast support outside of the classroom.

Now you see the intention of our teaching. Consider your part of it. If you teach three-year-olds, you won't be holding theological discussions, but you will need to convince the children that church is a good place to be, that other children have rights, and that adults can be trusted to help them when they have lost control or self-esteem.

If you teach second- or third-graders, you may be overwhelmed with the amount of story material you think should be covered. Don't worry about "covering" anything. There's time next week and the weeks after for you. There is next year and the years after for them. What is important at the moment is interest, wonder, and understanding of what is learned, not the amount you think you have taught.

When you meet for the first time with older children or young people, you may find that some have keener perception than you about some matters of faith or meaning of Scripture. If you want to give everlasting gifts to your students, encourage them and learn from them. Your job is to arouse an appetite for learning and to provide a variety of good food. You don't have to put it on the spoon.

You are probably bothered somewhat about how to maintain order. We will talk about that all the way through the book. It is a crucial and subtle matter. It is enough to say now that some days you will go home with alleluias in your throat and sometimes you will have a hard time getting your chin off your instep. But while you are down there, try to remember that there isn't a competent teacher anywhere who has not felt the same way.

CHAPTER 1
First Things First

❧

Getting ready to teach for the first time is like preparing for a hurdle match. The first thing you do after you have cleared the track is put the hurdles in order. In a horse show it is easy. You can measure the hurdles with your eye. Not so with teaching. What looms large in your mind's eye may be small when put next to something you didn't even know was there. Your questions are probably ones like these: What exactly do I do on the first day? How can I read, digest, and understand all of this biblical material? What do I do if I can't control the group?

Believe it; it's true—your first hurdle is *not* knowing

what to do on your first day. It isn't reading and understanding your curriculum resources or keeping your class from climbing out the windows. Those come later. The first hurdle is having the courage to be yourself and see your students as people too.

THE PERSON YOU ARE

Teachers, experienced or inexperienced, devise the most intricate ways of hiding their lack of self-confidence in the areas of teaching skills and subject matter. Sometimes those defenses become so much a part of our teaching that we assume roles. We become, heaven forbid, *types*.

Several years ago a group of exceedingly astute young people made a devastating analysis of their most memorable teachers. They were not aware of the indictment they pronounced upon us as they gave us labels, each one hitting the dead center of a weakness. One of the young people told about a man who at first couldn't be categorized. He didn't fit their patterns. Finally, one of the girls emerged from the slough and said, "Maybe he's a guy who can't be anyone but himself. He says, 'I don't know what Isaiah meant, but I'll tell you what I thought when I read what he said.' He's just natural." They added "ordinary person" to their list. He wasn't given the ribbon for Best of Show. They said no more about him. If they only knew what a tribute they paid the whole person by remembering him as a teacher.

Now, look at the others they found so easy to label. Most of us find ourselves here if we dare be objective enough.

THE MAGICIAN OR SANTA CLAUS

These teachers put on an act and hope that it is sufficiently interesting to maintain order and enthusiasm for the hour or two they meet. Some are well informed about methods and subject matter. They are the ones most likely to succeed. One generally finds them in preschool through second-grade groups. After that the spell is broken.

The magician has a smile on her face before the children come into the room. She hovers over the children at the door and asks them questions she is sure they can answer, the answers to which she does not hear or care to hear. It's her act, not theirs. The session proceeds on the strength of her personality. The children act in ways they feel will be pleasing to her. When she tells a story, she weaves a magic web, if she is good enough, and all eyes are on her. To get attention she says softly: "I want to see two little eyes, Johnny. Two sparkling, smiling brown eyes. There! Now we can hear a story, can't we?" She is not like Mother, who probably says, "If you're ready to be quiet, I'll tell you a story." The magician has a distinct charm—she's not real.

One of the most capable magicians of the church was a preschool teacher, now retired, who for many years had taught and been observed by others. She could make children dance like leaves, act like old men walking through snow, sit breathless until Tommy-of-the-story told his mother he lied. One day she was ill, and she was tired. The children were in various centers of interest when she began gathering them for singing, conversation, and story time. As usual, she pranced from one to another with her magic wand. "Presto!" she sang and one by one each child responded to a gentle tap on the head. All but one boy. He would have none of it. Normally she would have ignored him rather than lose face. This day she lost her smile, she raised her voice, and shouted, "Go and sit on the rug. *Right now!*" The silence that fell on the room was incredible. From then on nothing succeeded. The boys and girls were quiet but not responsive. Their magician had turned into a witch. In truth, she had merely stepped from the stage to humanity, but the children had come for the show.

The magician impresses adults too. Many a neophyte teacher watches and wishes to be the artist she sees at work. But remember, you have to have a great deal of energy and a considerable amount of confidence in your acting ability to be a first-class magician.

The Santa Claus is nowhere near the perfectionist his female counterpart is. He loves children and wants them to love him. They gather around and sit on his lap. He pays little attention to curriculum resources or classroom procedures. He is the center of attention and will do anything from rope tricks to passing out suckers to maintain the center. Most of the Santa Clauses in the church do more good than harm. They simply don't worry about what their worshipers are learning. One important thing that generally gets across to the children is that grown men in their church like them and want them to be there.

THE FOOTBALL COACH

Both men and women are in this group, and if they are well informed and unafraid, they make very good teachers of third-graders and older. Coaches have teams and, at best, they pose questions and problems for which the teams have to struggle for solutions. Coaches let them make mistakes and discover their errors themselves. Coaches ask more questions in order to help and offer more resources rather than answers.

A good coach assumes that everyone is on the team and ready to work out. Most of them are not too patient with those who don't want to play. When you see a child sitting on a chair in the hallway staring at his knees, you can be almost certain he was thrown out of the game in a coach-led class.

There are coaches who never get to serious work. These are men and women who, though interested in developing a team, don't get past sports, social activities, and wails about unfair parents. It's very likely that they are afraid of losing their status as coaches if they begin teaching the class. Instead they let the students determine the content completely. Discipline problems exist here too, but these coaches are more apt to ignore the problems and endure the disturbance. Nothing important is happening anyway, and they know it. You might think they would feel like failures, but most of them don't. They have never realized the significance of their jobs. Unfortunately, even those children and young people who are not interested in learning know that they are calling the shots. Unlike the Santa Claus described previously, the coach who doesn't play an important game holds little esteem in the minds of the students. They are older, have been to school, and have come to expect learning along with loving, even when they think they don't need either.

One of the most proficient coaches now teaching

admits with refreshing candor that without his ability to *make* his boys and girls work for *him*, he would be a total failure. He worries sometimes about those who drop out of church school when they no longer have him sitting on the bench expecting them to play ball. They miss him and they miss the team. He wants to teach them to be self-starting students, but he would have to give up his position, and he would miss that.

Good coaches are criticized for building team spirit, not school or church spirit. It is undoubtedly true, but more often than not, the criticism comes from those unable to do as well. No minister would be remorseful should the entire middle and upper schools be taught by skillful coaches.

THE BEST FRIEND

Men and women with humility and a sensitivity toward the minds and needs of others sometimes cast themselves as best friends. Some of our most competent teachers in the areas of independent study and research started out that way. Unlike the coaches, they are most interested in relating to persons individually and becoming important in the learning process. They say things like: "Let's find out together. . . . I hope you will report next Sunday. We all want to know. . . . I'll show you how to use this book."

When best friends excel, they do so because they have the ability to interest every person in the study material. They are acquainted with a variety of resources that are available to the students, and they have genuine concern about each person's development as a teacher.

When best friends fail, they are the first to know,

because their offer of friendship is either turned down or shown to be insufficient reason to get a class in a mood to study. The reason they know they are finished is that while they were busy relating to one individual, ten or twelve others were playing catch with the eraser, shaving the paint off pencils, making paper airplanes, and throwing all three out the window. They have several alternatives: they may quit, they may come back in a new role, or they may decide to be themselves. Upon being themselves, they risk, as do we all, not being able to do the job. More best friends quit or teach only a year than any other of these so-called types. Why? Because without order, regardless of the devious manipulation we may employ to get it, we cannot teach and few can learn.

A young seminary professor whose great satisfaction and gift is working with graduate students on the research necessary for their dissertations, reports unashamedly that he was not only a washout as a day school teacher but was the only student in the history of his seminary known to repeat "fieldwork." He was running an after-school club for fifth-grade boys who ran him. It's hard to be a best friend and be successful. Probably the ones who are don't need the label.

The Mother or Father

These people are in charge of a family, not a class. Normally they are found in preschool through third- or fourth-grade groups. They maintain order and leadership by establishing family rules or standards. The first day the children are told, "Everybody helps. . . . It is my time to talk and your time to listen. . . . We will wait until the other person is finished speaking. . . . Our room is our special place in the church." When new children join the family, the host group learns "Everyone is welcome," and then repeats the old slogans to newcomers.

Teaching the family something beyond the standards is quite possible, for order is well on its way. The family exists only as a means to organize and control the group. Some of the most effective teaching and some of the most blatant examples of adult domination and child fear have taken place in the confines of the church school family. When the standards are few, reasonable, essential, and understandable, the children are not afraid of forgetting them. They make sense. They become a way of life and the little family can go on to learn what is intended and expected. The danger in the system is the temptation to substitute the organization for the teaching content. The rules become the subject matter of everything that is done and the teacher is both enactor of the law and its enforcement officer.

A woman who has organized first-graders into families for about thirty years and has been applauded for doing so has often warned beginning teachers of the temptation on any Sunday at any moment to become master puppeteers, calling on the children to please rather than learn to think and act responsibly.

Being a church school mother or father may be healthy and reassuring to young children. But remember to ask yourself each time you remind the children of an old rule or establish a new one: Is this rule for their benefit or my convenience? Once in a while you'll surprise yourself at your answer.

The Day School Teacher

Children and young people can smell the chalk dust the minute a day school teacher begins teaching the class. And probably it's because seasoned professionals aren't afraid of children or what children think of them. They already know they can teach. It may surprise you to find out that all day school teachers are not accomplished church school teachers. Some few have the feeling that church education is different, that because it is voluntary and only weekly not much need be taught. These men and women teach church school as they were taught it, not as they teach children during the week.

A great many day school teachers in our churches have helped raise the teaching competence of whole schools, as well as the morale, by teaching well, allowing people to observe, and encouraging the beginners among us.

The Second Lieutenant

You know them even without their uniforms. They're both men and women and they run military school, not church school classes. Behind every straight line at a drinking fountain, on a field trip, or at the door of the sanctuary stands a second lieutenant. Generally they teach older children and young people.

At their best, second lieutenants can assume the leadership of groups of seeming renegades and in short order have them poring over Scripture, assisting in worship, and mobilizing a churchwide service project. That kind of military personnel has one characteristic over and above any of their field tactics that gives them the ability to mold and activate groups. They like the little soldiers, and their way with them is secretly a joke.

The difficulty comes with second lieutenants who run their part of the army with stern, tight controls because they are afraid of those they are teaching. Even if their students aren't afraid of them, they never learn self-discipline, because it's too much fun to get away with something and leave the officer in charge powerless to find the culprit.

There is a sturdy quality about most second lieutenants and many of them do innovative teaching inside their rigid behavioral requirements. But if you decide to be one, sleep a long time Saturday night. You have to be strong, vigorous, and wide awake.

Well, that's the list the teenagers made plus a hard look at each of us. No one can tell you how to be yourself, but the suggestion is made, because it's a good bit easier in the long run to begin right where you live. Use any idea you see, remember, or just read about that is natural to you. You may be a second lieutenant with a football coach's team or a magician who runs a family. When we talk about curriculum materials, you'll see even more clearly the necessity to choose your techniques and approaches to suit the person you are and the persons you teach.

THE PERSONS YOU TEACH

The first day you see your students in the same room reacting to you, one another, and themselves, you'll look at them, and by the end of the session you'll have made snap judgments about each one. You may not remember them by names and faces, but the impressions of the individuals will be with you. You won't have to work at it; they'll be there. By their behavior they will be known.

"I know it all" speaks up first. Occasionally you meet someone who does know more than he or she is expected to and lets you know it immediately. If you're teaching young people, you'll find a few, quite likely, who know more than you do or think more deeply about what they don't know. You probably won't find them on the first day and you'll be glad when you do. They will teach you.

Most of the identifiable "I know it alls" are "I don't want to be heres" in disguise. The others who speak out are the "I want to knows" and "I want to pleases." We'll get to them later.

Often the "I know it alls" are shunned or ridiculed by the rest of the class. They are loners to begin with and, for all we know, may have adopted the pose as a defense. (If you think people don't like you, give them a reason and relieve the initial wondering in your own mind.)

You may not like the know-it-alls at first. But before you relegate them to the society of the unloved and unlovely, put on their moccasins and walk for awhile. When the shoes pinch, ask yourself, What do I need and want more than anything else in this world? You may see through the behavior to persons you would like to get to know; and that will make a difference in your teaching.

"I couldn't care less" is what many of us think of as a discipline problem. People are never problems. People present problems, solve them, or make them worse. On the first day, the "I couldn't care less" students dare to defy you, laugh out loud at others' mistakes, and cause elbow-to-elbow and under-the-table trouble that puts someone else in the defendant's chair. They are leaders in their own way and can take the whole class with

them. The secret in getting them to work for good rather than ill is to find out why they couldn't care less. Sometimes it's because they've passed these tests and are caring for far loftier things. Or perhaps they've failed so many times, they don't know how to care for anything. The important thing to remember is that they are leaders, and you best get them on the side of learning. You can do it only by getting to know them, finding out what they like to do well, and letting them do it. In other words, find out what they really care about.

"I want to please" generally does. He or she will be "good" the first day, because you need a few like that. They answer questions as they hope you want them answered. Their thinking is not deeper than yours and their responses depend on what they have learned is pleasing at home and at church school. Over and over new teachers have gone home after the first day thankful for those who want to please. They kept the class from bedlam. But, and this may surprise you, by Thanksgiving most of those teachers want to shake them from their chairs and shout, "Think, you parrots! Think!" There are many reasons a child or young person wants to please, and some are so deep we cannot touch them. But for the rest we are to blame, because in our weakness we encourage them to be "good" and to give us the answers we want to hear.

"I want to know" can get under your skin. He or she is curious, sometimes argumentative, challenging, and dubious of your conclusions. "I want to knows" are generally in fifth grade or above, but now and then they appear as worried old men and women in kindergarten.

The best you can do in teaching them is to free them from your own limitations, give them resources beyond yours and the rest of the class's, and afford them the luxuries of wonder and finding out by themselves. Many a minister or professor has been an "I want to know."

"I wonder" has unfinished business concerning church and church school. Occasionally this quester shows up in the kindergarten. More often we don't recognize the breed until second or third grade. These children are doubters for one of several reasons. They may have learned too early that the devout are not always merciful or even honest. Some may have been exposed to a teacher who couldn't leave room for doubt and questions or a parent who doesn't care at all about their intellectual journey. Those who wonder about their doubts are tender souls. They are the poets and philosophers among us. To keep them in the household of faith we need to receive their questions without disapproval, make unashamed declarations of our own beliefs, and be willing to discuss their unbelief with them. If you're lucky enough to have an "I want to know" and an "I wonder" in the same class, do your best to help them be friends.

"I don't want to be here" belongs to a club whose members almost always must. Their parents may be teachers who arrive early for church school, attend worship afterward, and mingle with others at a social time before going home. Sometimes "I don't want to be here's" are children of the pastor who unconsciously has made the church an extension of the home. The children may regard it as family turf with family rules. On

Sundays, they react to losing the rights to the land upon the invasion of an alien society.

If they sulk in their chairs and refuse to participate, you will have time to think of ways to make your session with them tolerable if not interesting. But, if they play catch with their chairs and hide in the supply cabinet, you will be forced to take action. They are likely to thrive on responsibility, especially work they are expected to accomplish on their own, possibly before you get there. If their behavior is a legend in the congregation, you may need the help of one or two adults to be their companions and to take them out of the class if need be. Do not let them daunt you.

"I like it here better than school or home" regards the church as a haven. Several children from one family may take to life in the church in the same way. Apart from the church they may have a reputation for terrorizing young children and appearing calloused in encounters with their peers. But for unknown reasons the church or your class has become the place where they dare be their vulnerable selves. Find significant responsibilities for them, things they can do without failure, and show appreciation for work well done. They probably will not relate well to other students who may have experienced quite another aspect of their personalities or who perceive them as risky associates at best. Within the limitations of time and circumstance, help the whole class to work together in the interests of others so that all of them can point to one memorable task they accomplished together. You don't want the church building to be a safety zone unless life in it can prepare the fugitives for a compassionate life outside it on the busy thoroughfares and crossroads we all travel.

Those are some of the snap judgments you may make on your first day with some hints of what lies beneath the overt behavior. Now, one of the most worthwhile mental exercises you can engage in is a game called "What will I do if...?" Think of situations in your classroom caused by the behavior of any one of the students described above. How will you meet them? What will you do? When you've finished that bit of mental role playing, complicate your problem by imagining situations where two students lock horns, and ask yourself the same questions all over again. You'll be surprised how prepared you are for your first day if you've spent your preparation in resolving concrete situations rather than in nursing nebulous fears.

The curriculum resources you use and the effort you exert to make them live will be wasted if you don't wrestle with the person you are and the persons you teach. What you and they see on their first day is the clay God gave us. What you and they see later is that same clay hardening and being molded at the same time. The size and the beauty of the vessels produced depend a great deal on you and the teachers around you.

Chapter 2
Tools You Have to Work With

When day school teachers agree to teach, they sign contracts. Sometimes teachers in the church do, but most often they don't. What we have in the church is a covenant—an agreement, a pact between God and the people. God says, "You are my people. Keep my commandments." We say, "We are your people, God. We'll do it."

The person or committee asking you to teach lives under the covenant and is inviting you to also. The church promises and you promise. You can count on this pattern all the time you teach: keep a promise; expect a

31

promise. You are never alone teaching in the church.

You can expect printed curriculum materials. They furnish the content and many suggestions for teaching it within a total program—the curriculum of a local church. Materials are not the curriculum. They are an important part of it.

The materials you use are part of an organizational system of a particular number of years. It's helpful from time to time to take a look at the chart—curriculum materials always have charts—showing the sequence of the study your church has adopted. It can give you the feeling of contributing something, but not everything, to the knowledge and attitudes of those in your class.

When you've been given all the materials you need to begin teaching, the place to begin is the teacher's guide or course book, or the magazine for teachers. Whatever its title, it contains the teaching plans. It explains the use of all the materials in relation to what you do in preparation for and in teaching your group. There are three different ways the teaching plans are presented:

1. By dated session plans
2. By undated session plans
3. By units you schedule yourself

Look at the teaching plans you have been given. When you determine which type you have, read that section of this chapter. It will only confuse you to read all of them.

THE DATED SESSION PLANS

Since the beginning of church curriculum resources for children, dated session plans have been published.

These plans appear in a periodical—often called a teacher's guide—with suggestions for what you might do for forty-five minutes or longer each week. Generally the magazine comes quarterly. The content is divided into units of study that may continue into the following quarter. For example, in a year when Advent begins on November 29, a September–November issue would begin the unit and a December–February magazine would have the other three Advent sessions.

Most of the dated session plans are written in a style that would lead you to believe that if you could memorize it, you could follow it in detail. Suggested conversation as well as study questions are given in the order in which the writer and editor think best for the age group and most church situations. In truth, no one can follow the suggested plan exactly. Each individual and each group has ways of reacting to learning situations that make it necessary for each teacher to adapt the plan during preparation and on the spot while teaching. If you teach where attendance is sporadic, continued projects may be a meaningless waste of time, but with regular attendance, continued projects may serve as a review and an occasion for deeper thought for your group.

This is not to say that plans are useless. They are guides, not taskmasters. The content of a unit is divided into a prescribed number of sessions and presented in a variety of ways in order to avoid monotony and to encourage learning. In your adaptations, you would do well to work toward those ends too.

Many of the difficulties in the use of weekly plans such as these come from a teacher's unwillingness to adapt to the situation and to the learners. It takes time and thought to vary from the original and still have a respectable plan for use. It takes experience too. No one can tell you on paper what to do with the plans you are given. But the most experienced, mellowed, veteran teacher would say, "Go ahead. Try. Make mistakes. Learn."

Along with your session plans you have a variety of learning aids. They vary from resource packets of pictures, projects, audiotapes and videotapes to less ambitious but equally useful picture folios. You may also have an age group manual, a hymnal, sometimes a service or prayer book, and students' books or leaflets. The range of learning aids is mentioned because they are referred to by name in your teacher's guide and there is no stumbling block more effective than title after title of books, packets, projects in packets, pictures, and hymns you cannot find. Become acquainted with everything that is rightly yours. Stay on your toes, though, and keep your eyes open, because some items change every quarter while others are annual offerings.

One final word of caution should be sounded before you get too far into your teaching with dated session plans. There is almost always more than enough to do in a given session. Don't feel you have to complete everything. Look at the purposes or objectives and decide which techniques put forth are best for you, your group, the time, and place.

A teacher of five-year-olds who also teaches teachers through observation in her class is adamant about keeping calm when the children choose to move somewhere between slow and stop. She says, "Yes, I said we would go for a walk, but we'll have to do that next week."

One Sunday the group was assembled around a large poster each had contributed to, when the noise in the hallway told her that time was up for the day.

"Oh, my," she said, "It's time to go home, and we haven't even had a prayer today."

"That's all right, Mrs. Johnson," one of the boys said. "We'll have to do that next week."

THE UNDATED SESSION PLANS

Churches with a variety of teaching times for children, young people, and adults have found undated teaching materials useful. They can be used in conventional Sunday morning sessions, weekday groups, vacation church school, short-term study groups and extended, ungraded church school sessions.

Their real advantage was at one time a criticism of dated session plans. They do not change until a major revision takes place. This means that if you intend to teach for a few years or to help a beginning teacher in a couple of years, you should write notes to yourself in your course books about successes and failures, amount of time allowed for projects, content that aroused curiosity, and where you acquired some of the materials suggested. It stands to reason that the second time you teach the material, your familiarity with it will free you to innovate, observe learning problems in individuals, and evaluate your own performance.

No matter how detailed the instructions are or how many suggestions and alternatives are presented in the session plans, you have to adapt to your group, your teaching area, and yourself. It is expected that you do. Some of the undated materials for teachers are written as if one teacher is talking to another, giving hints on how to adapt in a specified situation. Others are written to suggest that the teachers are planning together and eventually come up with procedures that suit them. These are devices to teach you the uses of the materials and possibly to convince you that they *can* be used! These devices can become very tiresome if used to excess, but they carry enough freight so that you'd be wise to read them.

One of the promotional slogans used by some of the consultants when undated material was about to come to the churches was, "You are neither ahead nor behind the other teachers. We all go at our own pace." In a conversation at a teacher's meeting one night, it became evident that a man teaching third grade was getting perilously close to shepherds, angels, and stables with Thanksgiving yet to come. The other teachers bombarded him with questions. He always finished with time to spare, he said. No, he hadn't taken the class to see the sanctuary as suggested. No, he hadn't asked a church officer to visit. No, they didn't learn the songs. A teacher can go at his own pace and not use the material given him. True, the man was neither ahead nor behind the other teachers. He wasn't even playing their game.

To "adapt" means to shape what is given to fit your needs. It does not mean to substitute what is there with a totally unrelated program. Honest experimentation by qualified people is being done here and there all over the country in an effort to custom-make resources for one church's use in a total curriculum. It is not an easy job, and those who thought it was offered stones to people crying for bread.

It is difficult enough to be judicious in adapting what is there. Leave curriculum development to the experienced, and concentrate on being a capable teacher.

When you receive your course books, student materials, class packets, and whatever else is given you, check to see that you also receive any current literature from the denomination that helps you and the other teachers plan the year's schedule and adapt the materials to fit your calendar.

UNITS YOU SCHEDULE YOURSELF

Teachers are not expected or invited to choose the basic educational resources used in the school. That choice is made by other leaders in the church and approved by the official board. But with some resources you have choices within the choice your church has made.

You may decide to use a Bible skills unit for the month of September while another teacher begins the autumn season with the stories of Abraham, Isaac, and Jacob. That is just the beginning of your game of choices within a choice. It is best not to play it as a variation of solitaire, and it is always better to plan a whole year rather than one unit at a time.

Make use of your covenant relationship here. Ask for (1) assistance in planning from your minister or lay leaders in the congregation, (2) a planning meeting for all teachers, (3) an assessment by the minister or lay leaders of the plans you have made by yourself.

Use the church calendar as you plan. Your class belongs to the whole church. You can usher the members of it into congregational life and have a good time doing it. There are baptisms to witness, Lord's Suppers to attend, ordinations and installations to watch, anniversaries, festivals, all-church projects, visits with guests from other countries. You need not be the shepherd at each event, but it is your planning and your persistence that will enlist adults and young people as advocates of children as participants in worshiping, learning, working, and having fun together at church.

Take possession of the year's schedule once it is finished even if you are teaching only four out of nine months. It is not just your experiences with the children you are to be concerned about; it is their experiences in the congregation. In Bible study, congregational worship, and our compassionate relationships to others, the church is engaging in intentional memory building. In twenty years, what will your class members recall of this year you plan for them? How will your work affect their enthusiasm for next year or some time as imminent as next week?

NEW TOOLS

You need not be a computer whiz to make use of computer science in your teaching. If you are, your congregation can use your gifts of imagination and competence. Your denominational offices are venturing in appropriate ways to offer a vast variety of educational resources by way of computer technology. The possibilities appear to change almost daily; the range of useful probabilities changes less often—always with new discoveries and inventions.

The time is almost here when communicating with computers is as much a part of our lives as television. Many companies are producing computer Bible games, but a word of warning: Remember your covenant relationship and your freedom of choices within the choice of educational resources made by your congregation. You may be confronted with advice, values, and dogma in contradiction to what you have been teaching and quite different from the values and doctrines of your denomination. Be alert to the difference between proclamation of the Scriptures and seductive infomercials for a less demanding way of life!

ON THE JOB WITH OTHERS

Now that you know about curriculum resources in general, you're going to have to find out about yours in particular. Read the words, look at the pictures, examine activity and resource packets. Sing the songs if there are any. Singing helps release tension built up while worrying about how you can possibly do everything that is suggested. Your materials tell you over and over in many ways that you must choose what fits you, your class, and your situation. That's where your real job starts—with you, your class, and your situation—*after* having become familiar with the standardized tools many people in many churches are using.

Most denominations have devised ways to help congregations choose materials. You'll hear about these people later, except for one woman whose game you might play now. She was in a church in a very large state on the Pacific Coast, where the body of teachers and administrators were most unhappy with the product they had ordered from their denomination. She had the choice of either an ugly display of open warfare where she might lose for lack of numbers or an opportunity to teach something about the people there, the people they taught, and the situation they had helped create.

She called the game "Documentation," a less offensive way of saying, "Prove it." Here are the directions:

> Each player is given a sheet of paper with two columns, one "Objections" and the other "Documentation." The curriculum resources are set before the players. Any number can play. For every documented objection approved by the other players, a player gets ten points. The winner gets to be the church school superintendent, ex officio member of the Christian education committee, and chair of the curriculum appraisal committee (newly formed), and has the privilege of ordering, opening, and distributing the materials chosen.

The game was played as it was intended, in jest. An explosive, cantankerous man was slated for winner at the beginning, the players competing against one another, rather than the consultant they had come to push against the wall.

The consultant looked over the shoulders of the players, giving encouragement. "Now that objection," she said at one point, "can be documented. Try this book"

"But I teach sixth graders. That's for adults," the man answered.

"You want to *win*, don't you?" she asked. "Get out on the field and play!" The man became familiar with another aspect of curriculum resources, something beyond the group he was teaching.

When the game was over, so was the bitterness. But

the consultant was not finished. The entire group had discovered that they had contradictory objections, that anything could be documented or disproved, and that no one at the meeting was familiar with either the materials he or she taught or those which were taught by others, all part of one educational system.

"What are you going to do about your teaching?" she asked. "Are you ready to make resolutions?" They were, and they did:

1. Look at the total scheme for all education in the church.
2. Find your place in it as teachers and learners.
3. Become thoroughly acquainted with the materials.
4. Consider and study the possibilities for change in schedule, room arrangement, involvement in the church, and in your own teaching techniques.
5. Study together.

Who knows what they actually did? Peter baptized many at Pentecost who asked, "What shall we do?" To this question he answered, "Repent and be baptized." All that is known is that one group looked at themselves along with their resources and found neither was perfect.

Educational systems are made up of people. Curriculum materials are conceived, developed, edited, published, and sold by people. Either we march against the others or in the same army for the same end. There is little to be gained in fighting holy wars with other Christians.

CHAPTER 3
The Room Where You Meet

Fortunate are the teachers and pupils who meet in rooms built and equipped for them. Some discipline problems would never arise if the room were not full of diversions or forbidden objects. Other problems would be far simpler to solve if there were not twice as many warm bodies present as the room should hold.

It isn't too difficult to find a room for an adult study group in a church. Finding suitable room for the Christian education of children is far from easy in most churches. Everyone has to work at it, even the group that has always used the room with the rug in it.

You won't be able to do too much about choosing a room when you are asked to teach. The room will be assigned, and unless you have plenty of good reasons and unusual powers of persuasion, you'll undoubtedly take what you get. What you do with it is up to you.

The younger the children, the more room they need. Two-year-olds don't sit on chairs for too long a time at home, and they don't change their behavior at church. They need space to run and a warm floor on which to sit while playing by themselves alongside others the same age. They need toys to play with, as clean as or cleaner than the ones at home, and unless crayons are a part of their diet, they don't need those. With two-year-olds, start with space and add only functional equipment. Someone else may want the old piano anyway.

The older the persons, the more able they are to adapt to their learning environment. A group of senior highs or adults can work effectively in the south end of a parlor containing overstuffed furniture, two pianos, porcelain lamps, and mahogany end tables, without using any of them. At the other end preparations for a coffee hour can be going on quietly without disturbing the group. Comfortable chairs that can be moved easily are about all you need to begin with. Tables are useful only when tables are needed for something other than doodle sheets.

In between the two extremes of the roving two-year-olds and the sedentary adults are all the other learners. They fit into cubicles six feet by six feet, large assembly rooms, dining rooms, spacious schoolrooms, carpeted sewing rooms, kitchens, and multiple-purpose rooms. We'll take the rooms one at a time and see what ingenuity alone did with each one.

The Cubicle Six Feet by Six Feet

There were three of these rooms all in a row. They each had a chalkboard, a newsprint pad on a tripod, a bulletin board, a narrow supply closet, a table, and eight chairs. The rooms were to be used by third- through fifth-graders. The previous year the boys and girls had conducted themselves in such a way that not one teacher had returned for another year. The new teachers were aware of their problems before they began.

When they met at the church for the first time to plan together, their immediate concern was discipline. They would have to run a tight ship, one of the men said.

"Maybe that was the trouble last year," a woman countered. "They're held down so in school, you know."

There was more talk than action and very little planning done. As they were drinking coffee afterward in a large area adjoining the cubicles, a young man who had said very little previously asked, "Why don't we use this room for something?"

That started a discussion of a whole new use of the entire area.

The cubicles were used by small groups conducting research from reference books and magazines, doing cooperative projects on stewardship and mission, learning hymns, and doing hymn study, among other things. The "passageway," as it was called, was where half the group gathered at one time for discussion, reporting, hymn singing, and whatever else was called for in the larger group. There was no discipline problem too large for the teachers, who worked together well. Everyone had enough room, and everyone was busy doing something worthwhile.

The Assembly Room

The second- through fifth-graders had this two-story resounding room that had at one time been the sanctuary and now is used for young people's parties and children's Christian education. Sometimes the children sang, prayed, and learned surrounded by crepe paper streamers, corn shocks, Santa Clauses, cupids, or Easter bunnies, depending upon the time of the year and the reason for the party.

Each week the custodian set up a number of light-green screens to separate the children into small working groups. For some scientific reason having to do with the way sound travels, the screens magnified the sound. The din was eardrum piercing. The children were busy and not disorderly during the small group activities. But about halfway through the session, a buzzer sounded. As if jet-propelled, the boys and girls leaped to their feet, and like a fleet in formation, they pushed the screens and tables against the wall, slid the chairs to the front of the room, put them in rows, and sat down for a story, discussion, reports from the groups, and singing. Everyone listened to the story. The discussion had about a 2 percent participation on good Sundays, and hardly a soul past the second-graders in the first row heard the reports. Fatigue began to show on the children's faces and then it filled the room. When the time came for singing "Now Thank We All Our God," it sounded more like "Sweet and Low." Finally the buzzer sounded again, blood flowed once more in the children's veins, and they raced from the room.

Their teachers were working hard and getting very little accomplished. They thought long and hard about alternatives, knowing that you inevitably give up something to get something else. Their solution was to meet at four different times during the week, the second-graders utilizing the room at the regular Sunday hour.

"Do you miss your associations with the other teachers?" a weekday teacher was asked.

"We get together now and then just to congratulate ourselves. Our room is a surprise to us each time we come. The art work is *gorgeous!*" she exclaimed, waving toward a brilliantly colored mural at least ten feet long.

THE DINING ROOM

Dining rooms don't have to be a problem. Sometimes people make them so by placing stipulations on use of wall space, storage of school furniture, and use of the tables for art projects. Generally these problems are solved by going to battle or working against the odds. If the floor is warm and reasonably clean, children can work on newspapers and plastic sheets to do their painting, pasting, and assembling of projects. Even children who sit at desks or tables at school don't mind sitting cross-legged on a rug to converse, listen to others, and sing.

One nagging problem with big rooms furnished for purposes other than education is too much room without any of it belonging to the little learning community.

A couple new to church volunteered to teach fourth- and fifth-graders in the dining room. One Sunday after worship an elder introduced the two teachers to the rules of the room: Don't move the tables. Don't use the walls for anything. Don't leave materials and supplies in the room. The man and woman accepted their class space as a challenge and with considerable humor.

"We figured," the woman said, "we were new. Everything we did that was unconventional would be chalked up to our not knowing the ropes."

They didn't move the tables. They moved chairs out of a corner of the room that was carpeted. They didn't put anything on the walls. During the year, they "decorated" the walls of the corridor and stairway leading into the dining room. They left materials and supplies in the room, but no one knew it except the minister for awhile. They appropriated the drawers of a buffet that was almost empty when they examined it. The jigsaw puzzles, record albums, and quarterly teacher's guides from thirty years ago were given another home in the church.

When you make adjustments that require moving the contents of drawers or closets, you need the approval of someone who is authorized to give it. In this instance, the couple stopped the minister on her way through the dining room. "We could use the storage space in the buffet," the man said to her, "if you told us where to put these old record albums." They came with a solution rather than a problem. Try it.

The Spacious School Room

When this room was built, it was better equipped and planned than some day schoolrooms. Those were the days when families had 4.5 children on average instead of 2.1. Two teachers of kindergarten through first grade found the room "too big" for the ten to twelve children who regularly came. They complained to the superintendent who, with the minister, met in the room with the two teachers. What the four did was rearrange the room to cut out running space. That task led to removing pictures from the walls and decorating an art center around the built-in sink the teachers had covered over to avoid water fights.

The first Sunday of the new arrangement the children gathered on a 12' by 15' rug. They did some work at tables and chairs and at the art center. A dramatization began on the rug and spread throughout the whole room. As they returned to the rug for singing, Bible reading, and prayer, a girl said to one of the teachers, "I just *love* our new room!"

THE CARPETED SEWING ROOM

The problem was not that there were sewing machines in the room. The machines could be moved. It was the all-wool, broadloom carpet nailed to the floor that caused the trouble. First, the middle-schoolers used the room on Sundays and spilled punch on the carpet. They were moved to another location and the third-, fourth-, and fifth-graders were assigned the room. They dropped modeling clay on the rug and stepped on it. When the women came the next Thursday, they said it was like walking on gravel.

So the third-, fourth-, and fifth-graders were moved out and finally, the three- and four-year-olds were leased the property. The teacher was impervious to the warnings. The children painted. They worked with home-made salt and flour clay. They ran trucks across the carpet. They pasted up to their elbows. And no one said a word. The three- and four-year olds are still there in the sewing room on Sundays.

Why? The first teacher of that group was an impeccable housekeeper. The children painted with yards of plastic on the floor. They used clay in only one area, with plastic under the table. They pasted with abandon and then were sponged off as soon as they were finished. As far as the trucks going to and fro, they didn't hurt the rug as much as the legs of the sewing machine tables did. Somebody spilled apple juice at least once each Sunday, but apple juice blends in well with most carpets.

You won't always have to tread lightly when you use a carpeted room. Some churches have a refreshing openness toward maximum use of some tastefully decorated rooms. In a large church, there are four large rooms, all of which are used for receptions of one kind or another. There are carpets, grand pianos, some fine pieces of furniture, and breakable lamps. On Sundays the furniture is pushed back to make room for children ranging in age from four years through high school. Only newcomers are surprised to see this take place. But the tradition of the church is that those rooms outside of the sanctuary are for the church school, and the sanctuary is for them, too, whenever they come.

No members or groups in the congregation own any part of the church for themselves. Remember that. It's very easy to slip into the Three Bears Syndrome without knowing it. The first time you hear yourself saying, "Someone has been using my room!" you're well on your way to doing that.

There is a delicate balance between having a place children and young people call their own and owning that place alone. There was a time, generations ago, when children were threatened into "church behavior," because the church was God's house. The adults could do anything from having a surprise party for the minister

49

after congregational worship to holding a wedding reception for 500 talkative, effusive guests. But if a six-year-old boy ran down the corridor to meet his parents or, worse yet, stopped for a drink of water, he was given the word about just whose house he was in.

As the threat was heard less often, and as the children were welcomed into the church fellowship, respect, or at least decorum, followed in many instances. It's understandable. How would you have felt as a child if the adults in your house had freedom to wander from basement to attic, even into your room, and you were expected to stay in your bedroom until called? Wouldn't you be a bit clumsy, socially, when you were released?

It's so much less complicated and so much more honest of us to say:

- "*Walk* inside the church. There are people who don't see you coming and may trip over you."
- "No paper airplanes, David. None at all. Take it to the office and tell the secretary you want to put it in the wastebasket. Harvey will go with you."
- "I remind you again that it's very hard to get past fifteen high school students standing in the corridor. Go into the social room if you want to be social."
- "There's a special kind of clear tape we use after we tear pages in books. It doesn't rot the pages. Here. Mend the book."
- "The next time we go to church, no pencils. O.K.?"
- "Now, at the reception for new members, remember that two cookies are plenty. The cookies are

for everyone. I know you like them. But so do the grown-ups."

Share the church building, carpets and all.

THE KITCHEN

Don't laugh. Classes meet in the kitchens. A church may be small or big, but you can usually count on a kitchen. If you've been asked to teach three-year-olds and you're given the kitchen, trade with an adult study group whose members like coffee, or form one to lobby for you. Young children don't belong in the kitchen. There are too many dangerous diversions. It's a natural place for an adult class and not too bad for juniors and seniors in high school.

Kitchens vary. Some of the counters offer dandy writing space, but you normally need stools to sit on because the counters are high. If there is no other place but the kitchen for a children's class, it means that your church should reevaluate its present use of rooms.

If no class is using the kitchen, it is an excellent place for you to paint, fingerpaint, carve soap, work with clay that hardens, and make salt-and-flour topographical maps. Anything that's messy should be near running water. If your room is not, the kitchen is the place to be.

Gas stoves, knives, and other equally dangerous culinary equipment should either be out of reach or watched. If you don't work with other teachers, you'll do well to ask one parent for every three preschoolers painting and one for every five elementary children. This would not be so were you not in a kitchen. For that reason, give the responsibility of specific children to specific adults while you are still in your teaching area. Call them families, clubs, or groups, but make them aware that they belong to one another.

Once in a great while there is an opportunity to cook and, more often, to bake. We'll talk about substitute teachers later, but this is one place they can step in with ease.

In one midwest church, a call came out for food for families caught in a flood. The adults had already housed families. The teenagers had all been excused from school to fill sandbags. Only the children had not participated. The teachers had planned a meeting for the middle of the week after the flood, but on Sunday they asked the children what food they could bring the next week. Some of the flood victims were in the classes. Many ideas came forth. But one second-grade boy who was still living in his wet house said, wistfully, "Don't you think cookies would be nice?" That did it. The class decided to bring cookies, until the teacher said, "We can *make* them in the kitchen." Those children worked Saturday afternoon and Sunday morning, loving their neighbors while making them cookies.

If you try cookie baking, use overnight or prepared dough. Rolling is fun, but it makes the cookies tough. Cutting cookies, putting them on baking sheets, and taking them off when done, is quite enough. Fifth- and sixth-graders can put them in shock-proof packages.

OTHER IMPROBABLE PLACES

What can you do with a middle school class in the dark, dingy corner of the basement? Well, there are some ideas, but one beats all. The young people might have felt, justifiably, that they were outcasts, but the teacher had done his homework. The first three units of study were on the early church. The group learned that the sign of the fish directed people to the Lord's Supper and worship. They painted fish on the floor leading to the basement corner.

Many curious people throughout the week followed the fish prints and found only a dark corner with a low ceiling. Meanwhile, back at the middle school ranch, there was a boy in the class named John. He was six feet tall in September. By October it was obvious that he'd have to bend over to get into the room. By then the class had immersed themselves in early church history and had learned about the catacombs as a secret place for worship. As John ducked in one day a bit late, one of his classmates said, "Welcome to the catacombs." After that the area became known as "John's Catacombs," and bore a sign to tell others, "We Are Christians Under Fire."

Dark corners are not recommended as classrooms by or for anyone. But if you draw the short straw and get a difficult room not intended for human habitation, take a good look at your whole church. Maybe there is a better space no one has thought of using. If there is not, you have a few alternatives. Use the space given you and have fun with it.

If your room is the old stage, be thespians. Dramatize almost everything you study, and when you're a real working troupe, visit other classes by prearrangement.

If it's a foyer your group is in, with people passing through or where only low voices are permitted because of the preaching and singing next door, pick up your books and Bibles and go to someone's living room. You can't teach in bedlam or in what is expected to be a vacuum.

You have been asked to be a teacher. If you can't teach because of the peculiarities of the space you have been given, let it be known, even if you are not armed with an alternative.

Be cheered by the spirit of some of our most seasoned, down-right salty veteran teachers who often dramatize the needs of their groups or the unintended thoughtlessness of others.

In a church where no room was built for a teaching area as such, a woman taught kindergarten for twenty-five years in a large room with seven doors. "It was all right when I was young to have people go through," she said. "But I haven't the patience anymore to put up with adult conversations in the back of the room while the children and I are getting ready for a story."

The next Sunday, the adults gathered to chat in the back of the room as they had before and the gracious, silver-haired old pro swung into action. When the class finished their project, the teacher walked to the back of the room. "Friends," she said, "the children made a guest book today. Won't you please come up and sign it before you leave?" Each person signed the book, was introduced to the boys and girls as a special visitor, was asked what he or she did in the church, was thanked for the visit, left by one of the seven doors, and never again interrupted.

MULTIPLE-PURPOSE ROOMS

You have probably gathered by now that few rooms are not multiple-purpose rooms. There are, however, rooms that were built to be multiple-purpose. They didn't fall into the uses; they were planned. In a small church, a large room was built and equipped with a vast storage area underneath an adjoining, elevated room. On Sunday, the children use the room. Their furniture and equipment are all put away in the afternoon so that the young people can use it for recreation on Sunday evening. Monday is the custodian's day off. Tuesday, tables are set up for women's service sewing. Wednesday, everything is removed and the floor is scrubbed. Thursday, Alcoholics Anonymous meets. Friday is shared by various adult groups, and Saturday is spent setting up the room for children to use on Sunday.

The advantage to a room like this one is that while you are using it, it does suit you. The disadvantage is that everything has to be put away and taken out by someone else. The teachers in the room described had several solutions to the problems of what to do with unfinished work and how to display what is finished. All uncompleted group projects were kept in a long chest used as a window seat. Individual paper projects were kept in folders, with each child's name printed conspicuously on a folder. Other individual projects had name labels on them. It was a lot of work, but it was effective. The teachers learned as time went on to start projects early, have working materials at hand, and work toward completion in one session. Adding to a group project each week was not difficult. It was individual project carry-over that was almost irritating in its detail. As the teachers became accustomed to planning the individual work so that it could be finished in a session, there were nowhere near as many folders to put in the chest. Displaying finished artwork and pictures used for teaching was made easy by using a few screens that stayed in the room and looked attractive.

Another kind of multiple-purpose room is that used

for preschool weekday programs, nursery care, and church school for three- and four-year-olds. The problem here is not space or suitability of the room to the children. It is supplies and sometimes equipment. If the church rents the rooms to a private enterprise, there may be equipment for them and equipment for you. More negative teaching has been done by having equipment in the room that boys and girls cannot use because it belongs to someone else. If it's there and you aren't supposed to use it, have it removed. If it cannot be removed, use it.

If the preschool program is run by the church, the equipment should be used by any preschoolers in the church's program. Some supplies may be kept separate and others shared. Meet with the weekday leaders and plan together what to do about supplies and equipment. We all have a tendency to be proprietary about our room, our supplies, our rocky boat, and our wall space. Just try for awhile to include all the groups using the room in the word "our." It has worked well. Can we who teach others to share, not teach ourselves?

CHAPTER 4
You Are Not Alone

Do you remember the story of the poor, little old woman who was coming home from town with her pig and what happened when she came to a stile the pig could not hurdle?

She asked a reluctant dog, stick, fire, water, rat, cat, and cow for help. Finally she met a farmer who fed the cow some hay so it would give milk for the cat to drink.

Then—
The cat began to chase the rat.
The rat began to drink the water.
The water began to quench the fire.

The fire began to burn the stick.
The stick began to beat the dog.
The dog began to bite the pig.
The pig jumped over the stile.
And the old woman got home that night.

Her trouble was not that the world was poorly organized. The woman simply didn't know where to go for help. When she found the instrument of change, the action was swift and effective.

Your initial search for help may be like hers, even if you ask help of the logical person to give it. No two churches function alike, no matter how similarly they are organized. Why? Because of people with their shortcomings and their gifts. No person can help you all the time. Get acquainted with the minister, officers, Christian education committee members, superintendent of the church school, your teaching team, parents, and several people who look like good substitutes. When you need help, decide who best can fill your need.

THE MINISTER

The typical minister doesn't exist. Those who think they know one are talking about either the one they liked best or the one they liked least and are measuring all others by him or her.

Some ministers are exceedingly interested and aware of what is going on in Christian education in the world, their denomination, and their church. They vary from scholars who are intent upon bringing biblical theology into the classrooms to superduper organizers who run clean houses of business during the week and play "pal" by sitting on the floor with the five-year-olds on Sundays.

From people within that wide range, you can get all sorts of help. They may be able to assist you with your study content, give you insights on methods you have not tried, give you books on techniques, and tell you about skills workshops or courses you can take. They may be listeners, too, who can help you help yourself. Their skills vary with their aptitudes and preferences.

Other ministers have a reputation for not caring about Christian education, and sometimes that is the truth. Far more, however, are for it but not with it. They are confounded by the increasing number of changes taking place and, without examining each for its life expectancy, wonder what was wrong with the great ideas the boards and agencies had last year. They seldom think of the organizations behind changes in Christian education as groups of people changing yearly by appointments, resignations, research, experience, and education.

These ministers vary from those who are able teachers of biblical, theological, and ecclesiastical content to those, unfortunately, who don't seem to be able to talk understandably about those subjects to anyone who didn't go to seminary with them.

Some words of caution are in order about deciding whether or not a minister is interested in you and your job as a teacher. Quiet persons are not necessarily aloof or disinterested. Sometimes these are the very people with perception sharp enough to cut straight through to the core of an issue whether it is theological, methodological, interpersonal, or organizational. They are the undiscovered giants of the clergy, and for the most part, prefer to remain in the wings of your performance.

There are also those men and women of the cloth

who have a low tolerance for trivia and who, rather than face anyone concerned with little details, simply remove themselves. One minister confessed to pretending, after three telephone calls from teachers, to be out, while, in reality, he was in his study preparing a sermon.

"The first woman wanted her Christmas tree cut in half lengthwise and plastered on the west wall. The second teacher was a graduate student who had forgotten to say anything about sending the film he used Sunday to the rental agency. And the third caller asked me if there was enough money in the treasury for *six paper punches*."

You should never be afraid to go to your minister to ask questions about your teaching, but sort out the questions first. Maybe one of the others whose job it is to help you is the person to ask.

Ministers more than anyone else in the church are given assumed personalities from remarkably little data. The director of children's work of a church ten times the size of the town she had grown up in asked her senior minister to do a series of study nights for experienced and new teachers. For fifteen years the story had been that he didn't care about the teachers. When he called their bluff, the meetings were well planned and well taught. The average attendance was seven. On the last night of the series, a woman who was a lawyer said, "You have given us so much to think about and not many answers. I wish more people had been here."

"College," he said in response, "is a teacher at one end of a log and a student at the other."

Of course, more people could have profited by attending. But teachers have the same exasperating faults everyone else has. "He isn't interested in what we do" may be a coverup for "I am not interested in what he can do for us" or "I can get by without his help."

Every minister knows this. Ask one.

THE OFFICERS

Anyone who thinks that the officers of a church are one monolithic bloc need only sit in on a meeting, especially one about how money is to be spent.

There are no generalizations about boards and committees in churches, and it's even hard to generalize about those in one church. Whatever they are like, however, they do determine policies that affect you. Even not acting at all is a form of policy making.

Where interest in Christian education is high, a group of teachers can ask for a total reorganization of the church school and get it. Where interest is low, it's hard to get a replacement for a blown-out light bulb.

You may find what you think are contradictory actions from your church officers. Usually these are the results of a lack of understanding, and at best, an articulate teacher or parent should act as spokesperson for those who want change.

In a church in the southeastern section of the country, there had been an active, productive Boy Scout organization for about ten years. Some of the boys were not church or church school attenders. At one period, many of the teenage boys in the troop were working for the God and Country Award. The scoutmaster and the young, new minister worked out a program for the boys, only to be reminded by an officer there were two rulings of long standing on the official books that stood in the way:

1. No child is permitted to come to church school

unless his or her parents attend congregational worship.

2. No child may attend congregational worship unless his or her parents accompany him or her.

Three men, all fathers (a Presbyterian, a Methodist, and a Southern Baptist), appeared before the official board. They did not criticize; they asked questions.

- "Where can children in this neighborhood go to church school if their parents are not interested in the church?"
- "How old are the children when they become members of the church?" (The answer was twelve.)
- "At what age may these children who are members attend church without their parents?"
- "At what age may a child who is not allowed to come to church, join the church?"
- "What is your opinion of the God and Country program as outlined?"

Discussion, argument, and a few explanations followed. The neighborhood had changed radically in the life of the church, but the rules had stayed the same. The young minister had been chosen because of his interest in the changing city.

At long last an elderly man said: "I grew up in this neighborhood, and I live in a better one. We made those rules because of the way we were. Things are different now, and we need new rules." The patriarch, having spoken, made a motion, which was seconded and passed.

You don't always have to present your concerns to the official body. If you are acquainted with a person who is on the board or committee, he or she can bring the issue to a meeting. This method is used far more often and is effective particularly in noncontroversial matters that are important simply because no one has thought to correct them.

One such matter was settled at a meeting by reading a note written on the back of a used envelope and passed to an elder at corporate worship:

> Dear Joe,
>
> If we had those dirty tumbling mats recovered, we could put them under the climbing apparatus in the kindergarten room and reduce the head injury rate to practically nothing. I'm almost out of Band-Aids.
>
> Dee

THE CHRISTIAN EDUCATION COMMITTEE

Most churches have a committee of the governing body or a separate board specifically for discussing and deciding on matters related to Christian education. Sometimes they are working committees, but most often they are advisory. The committees have been criticized for not being aware of what is happening in the church school and not deciding on positive action often enough. The criticism is undoubtedly justified in some instances, but before you make up your mind to complain *about* the committee, complain *to* it.

The very people who wish for more action and fewer words would be most surprised and perhaps uncomfortable if each Sunday they had visitors from the committee seeing the classes firsthand.

Find out who is on the committee and if it is organized so that a particular person is responsible for your age group. *That is the one to know.* Go to the store; don't wait for the store to come to you.

When you contact persons because something has come up too big for you to handle, be patient for several reasons:

- Committee members probably have regular paying jobs somewhere else.
- They may have to wait until the committee meets to work on your problem.
- They may not understand the issue the first time around and misinterpret it initially.
- They may vote you down.

If it's a matter of discipline and you find out that the persons cannot help you, dismiss the problem momentarily. There are others who can help. Providence puts people in churches and on committees for many reasons. Rejoice that the treasurer of a large corporation is behind your efforts all the way. He can get more things moving than three hundred retired school teachers can, even if third-graders in groups of more than two baffle him.

These people are like all of us—they make mistakes unknowingly. A most proficient former teacher of day school was a member of a Christian education committee in charge of elementary grades. She could substitute from nursery to sixth grade and do a creditable job, but on the committee her preoccupation was housekeeping. The "baddies" kept lost purses, offering plates, and pupil's books on piano tops. The "goodies" had a clean shop. She was never there when the teachers were and had no idea of the quality of the teaching apart from what the walls and shelves taught her.

One of the men who taught junior highs joked with her. "Good housekeeping never was a problem with me. I ignored it completely. Why don't you show the teachers how to teach and clean at the same time?"

"Not a bad idea," mused the minister, turning a gibe into a concrete idea. The woman's services were offered to any teacher or team in the elementary grades. The schedule for observing her while teaching each class in grades one through six was full within two weeks.

It isn't often that people want to teach in that many grades, even if they can. But there may be persons on your committee and available to the committee who might be able to teach while you watch. They do not come so that you may copy their every move. They teach so that you may watch both their techniques and the responses of the children. It is nothing short of amazing how much you learn in one session about the boys and girls you already know, by watching someone else teach them.

This is the kind of idea you might suggest if no one else thinks of it. There may be people you know who are accustomed to being observed in day school or church school who are no longer teaching regularly. They may not mind coming for a week or even longer, if you find you're learning from them. Work through the committee, not independently. It is an idea that could become a teacher education technique useful to the whole school.

One thing to keep in mind while working with the Christian education committee is that some of them are new at their jobs, just as you are. Generally, the people are chosen because of experience and interest, but more than a few times they have learned much on the job. Some of what they learn can come from you.

If the committee members decide to visit classes for their own orientation, it may make you and those with whom you teach nervous, addled, and jumpy. If you are not ready for visitors, say so. Tell them how you feel. It may be that they can learn from you in a way that will profit others.

It might be, however, that no one asks to visit—and simply comes. A former day school teacher who had taught for only a year gave invaluable assurance to teachers who had taught in her church for many years. She said, "I was twenty-one years old and teaching high school seniors who weren't too crazy about learning.

"The principal came panting into my room saying, *'The state and county supervisors are here!'*

"I was stunned by his frenzy. They weren't the British in 1775. They were people who either ran for office and won or were appointed by those who had. At best, they were master teachers; at worst, they were those who fled the classroom for administration. And in between, who is to know what they were?

"I said to myself, 'Well, kid, you're not the worst there is, and don't think you're the best they've ever seen. They won't notice you in all probability.'

"They didn't. They told me they liked the way I used those impossible window shades I hadn't touched out of fear for three months. Those shades snap at you, you know. Then they said, 'The noise in the room was constructive.'

"I remember sizing them up and saying to myself, 'I hope I never get good enough to be a superviser. It's an impossible job for a human being.'"

It may not be possible, and those who do it well do not find it easy. Be kind to those who try—they can help you.

The Superintendent of the Church School

The job of superintendent depends a good bit on the expectations of the church for its school, the capabilities of the teachers, the activity of the Christian education committee, and the amount of professional assistance available.

Some superintendents function almost in the way a director or minister of Christian education might, while others order, unwrap, and distribute curriculum materials. Even in one church, a series of superintendents over the years may perform in totally different ways.

No one can tell you exactly how superintendents can help you be a more effective teacher, but you can be fairly certain that knowledgeable or not, they want to support you.

At a Saturday leadership school recently, a man complained, "I teach week after week and nobody knows I'm there." What he meant, of course, was that no one was interested in what he did in his class. One can be left too much alone, feeling unappreciated rather than trusted. If it is the superintendent's job to see that there are enough teachers to go around, you can be sure that you are appreciated.

In many churches the superintendent is also a member or ex officio member of the Christian education committee. He or she may be your voice on the committee.

Superintendents are not generally chosen because they are excellent teachers. If they are good teachers and there are enough in the church school already, so much the better. But their real job is one of organization and coordination. As an elderly man in Tennessee said, "I tell them every fall, 'See me about the nuts and bolts. I'm a hardware man. The preacher is your theologian.'"

Here are a few matters the superintendent should be able to help you with:

- "The children leave their offering money in a basket. Sometimes the basket comes back. Sometimes it is in the office. Sometimes I can't find it at all."
- "At 9:40, someone came in to count our noses. At 10:00, a boy came in for our offering envelopes. At 10:15, Tom's father came to get him so that they could get to the game early. At 10:25, you brought in our youth magazines. Why can't we get together once and settle all our business with each other?"
- "My class would like to put on a puppet play for the younger children. Which Sunday is best for them? Where may we perform it? What time is best for everyone? It takes ten minutes or so."
- "We would like to be in church the next time there is a baptism. When will that be?"
- "Jim Hansen has a broken heel and will need help getting up here. When you see him come in, will you send word so that the boys can help him?"
- "Do we have any money for a Bible dictionary, a concordance, and a historical atlas? Will you order them or shall I?"
- "Where were the Christmas tree stands put last year?"

- "What time is it?"
- "Could you come in the week after next and tell the boys and girls what you do in the church?"

Don't be afraid to ask for legitimate things. Your superintendent's job depends somewhat on the requests you make. On the days you see him or her idle in the hallway, be thankful. People fall, get sick, want their mothers, spill, get their index fingers caught in bottle necks, and forget where they left their jackets. Your superintendent is there to handle many things.

YOUR TEACHING TEAM

Sometimes the whole children's division is led by new teachers. When this is so, you can decide to do things your own way. Each one helps the other. One has a good singing voice, another cooks up recipes for finger paint and clay, and still another can tell stories well. Whatever you've done in the past helps now. It helps everyone.

Occasionally a person accepts the responsibility of teaching out of duty, perhaps, and admits to not being able to do one thing well. The tendency of other teachers is to say, "Oh, come on! You don't know yourself. It's easy."

Well, it isn't easy. And if you are the one without talent, you are the one in trouble. You have to learn what you can do. There are two courses to follow. You can try everything—or do nothing. You will, without a doubt, have much more fun if you try everything, laugh at and learn from your mistakes, and rejoice with abandon at your victories. But if you are not ready for laughing at yourself, and many of us aren't, you need help.

Try the easiest thing you know first, even if it is not the best technique you think should be offered the group. Here is an example from the life of one who made it.

- "I was scared witless, I tell you, and I hated myself for it. Sixth-graders were my lot, and I didn't know *one*. I looked at my materials, and I said, 'I can't, I can't, I can't.' Then I saw a crossword puzzle. O.K., I know it was a review, but it gave me an idea. I write crossword puzzles for half my living. I made up one called 'Bible, Atlas, and You.' It was a hit, and it taught me what the class could do, what they knew, and what I had left to do as a teacher."

Most of us have no notion of how to make a crossword puzzle, but there are things we know how to do, and surely each of us can learn to do something we have not done.

- We all conduct discussion groups with our neighbors and friends.
- We dramatize each time we imitate another person.
- We work with clay each time we make pie crust or cookies.
- We paint each time the crib gets another coat.
- We tell stories each time gossip makes its rounds.
- We all know how to teach in one way or another.

If you know skill upon skill and your teaching mates do not, you are the helper, not the helped. Just because things come easy to you, you need not assume they are simple tasks for others.

A man who taught fourth-graders in day school told a group of church school teachers, "Don't worry. Just say, 'I am Mr. Nelson. I would like to know your names.'"

It sounded easy. A man just beginning to teach a seventh-grade class tried the approach. These are some of the names he got on the name tags:

- Hubert Hoover
- Hoobert Huver (They worked together)
- Charlie Brown
- Your Friendly Ford Dealer
- Paul Revere

Do not be deceived. Foolproof techniques are only safe against the foolish. Children and young people are not fools.

You may be a new teacher among experienced ones. They can make you feel comfortable, show you where things are, and explain the schedule. Or, unfortunately, they can make you feel as if you don't have a brain in your head. If the latter is true, prove that you are intelligent by being cordial, competent, and oblivious to their attitude. People who slight newcomers are very often afraid of what they might know or think should be done differently. It is their own brains the old-timers are worried about, not yours.

The supersensitive persons we will have with us always. Work around them and be kind; they are not likely to change. A young woman from Chicago tells about a year she and her husband spent in North Carolina, where she was asked to teach three-year-olds. The other two teachers eyed her suspiciously the first day, and before she had a chance to say anything, they made excuses for the noise the children were making, the disarray in the room, and their appearance.

"The only thing wrong in the whole room," she recalled, "was dirt. The next week I brought sponges and interested a few boys and girls in bathing dolls and wiping up the water they spilled.

"You would think that was harmless if not beneficial, but the head teacher said, 'We liked it the way it was.' And so it stayed."

People are no pettier in the church than anywhere else. They are simply more obvious there.

THE PARENTS

There are several reasons for getting to know the parents of the children or young people you teach. You want them to know what is being taught, why you teach the way you do, and that you are interested in them and their child. But the most important contribution they can make is knowing you well enough so that they are not offended should you call to talk about the child. There are many reasons you might want to call:

- The entire group is out of your control, and you need the parents' help to decide what to do.
- One child does not respond to conventional disciplinary measures.
- A three-year-old does not move a muscle below his eyelids between the time his father brings him and comes to get him.
- A four-year-old sits in the middle of a group of children reading them stories.
- A senior high boy learns from you that scholarships are available for higher education.

- You would like to have a generation gap panel discussion.
- You want someone who has been to the Middle East to talk with the fifth-graders.
- You need a substitute.
- Jane broke out in a rash after she had the fruit juice and crackers in the kindergarten room.

A good relationship with parents is essential at all ages, though it is not the same kind of relationship at each age level. Young children find a teacher's visit a great honor, whereas a teenager might question both parents' and teacher's motives for what looks like a pointless visit. As an eighth-grade boy put it, "She came to visit my mom with that awful, 'I'm having trouble with Dan' look."

Books have been written about the church-and-home relationship, but with all the ideas put forth for getting parents to the church and teachers to the homes, the same point comes through: You should know one another well.

YOUR SUBSTITUTES

There are two kinds of substitutes and two kinds only: those who know the material and how to teach and those who do not. We need both kinds because there are never enough of the former.

Those people in the church who do not want to teach all the time but are willing to attend planning meetings with you and keep current materials on hand make your absences from your class a worthwhile experience instead of a waste of time. You are fortunate if you have one such person on whom to call. If there are more, so much the better. You will probably not be responsible for finding your own substitutes initially, but if you know of persons who would help you, it is likely that they will be welcomed.

It is no longer easy for a teacher to come in and take over for another. Resources are not as prescriptive as they used to be. If the substitutes in your church are not acquainted with your plans, you would do well to have a few ideas on hand that supplement what you are doing rather than develop it in the way you planned. Here are some examples:

- Take the three-year-olds out to plant crocuses, or use the seeds in your cupboard to plant flowers inside.
- Take a tour of the church or neighborhood and have the class make a list of what they are seeing for the first time. If there is time, make a poster showing all of these things.
- Make tray and place mats for hospitals and convalescent homes.
- Read a story from a book kept on hand for substitutes.
- Bake cookies with second- and third-graders to give to an elderly shut-in or a homebound child.
- Discover how to find verses in the Bible from the books listed in the Table of Contents. Learn where the Old Testament and New Testament are. Find familiar stories.
- Learn how to use a Bible dictionary, an atlas, and a concordance. Test one another.

In your materials you will find occasional suggestions for projects that you have no time for but that would be helpful anytime. Save these for the substitutes. There may be days when for unforseen reasons you don't get to church school and there is no substitute. Any operation depending entirely on people to make a go of it is a calculated risk. You must not feel that you carry the whole burden of your students' Christian education. God acts in their lives and yours. You are not alone.

CHAPTER 5
Nourishment for the Asking

After a leadership school in Idaho, all workshop leaders were asked to give evaluation sheets to their students, people teaching in church school throughout the region. Most of them answered the questions in almost the same way. They had learned new things. They enjoyed their classmates. They hoped the school would be held each year. One evaluation sheet was different. It read, "I cannot answer the questions. All I know is that I came here to learn enough to begin teaching next September. Now, I want to be a 'career' church school teacher, and I want to be *good*. Where can I get more help?"

There is help outside your church, and this person had already taken advantage of one teacher education opportunity. You may not want to become a "career" teacher in the church school, but you may want to do as well as you can as long as you teach. One of the easiest things to do in teaching is to fail. And when we do, it is one of the hardest things to take. All of us know that because we have tasted failure. If some teachers haven't, they have been exceedingly quiet about it.

So where do you get more help? The logical places are not always the most evident to one who does not know the ecclesiastical form and order. Here are a few jobs performed by people who can help you.

DENOMINATIONAL CHRISTIAN EDUCATORS

Consultants for leader development, use of resources, or teacher education—call them by their peculiar denominational titles—are pivotal in a quest for more help in effective teaching. Sometimes they are master teachers, sometimes generalists, but their real function is to lead you to others who have a particular interest in and capacity for teaching the age group you are teaching.

Their work is regional and with local churches, but seldom with one teacher. The exceptions are in their correspondence with you and personal conferences by appointment. Sometimes pastors are unaware of the interest of some of the church school teachers in area events, and it doesn't hurt to be on the mailing list of the area office if such a service is offered.

Occasionally, requests come to area personnel that protocol and common sense demand be referred to someone else. One such request was from a teacher in a church of over 1,500 people with two ministers and a director of Christian education. He wanted to know who could give him additional help with his newly organized, revitalized younger youth program. The consultant was polite and brief in her reply, ending with, "I suggest that you talk again with your D.C.E. Since she was instrumental in the changes in your program, she can give you the support you need."

Most area Christian education consultants would like to give more personal, individual help than their schedules permit. Those who are employed as consultants have a region to serve. Many, however, are volunteers with other jobs. Their help to you is largely through the events you attend and the people you meet at them. Their purpose is to develop strong, intelligent leadership in their regions and wise choice and use of resources in the churches.

Master Teachers, Leaders of Leaders, and *Teachers of Teachers* are all names for people equipped to teach while others watch and then to discuss with the observers what was done and why. Some are former day school teachers, while others received their education almost entirely from people like themselves. They are courageous souls. It is most enjoyable to watch an excellent teacher at work, but trying to be an excellent teacher while twenty to thirty eyes look on is no joke.

We all learn a good bit about teaching from watching a good teacher at work, but before we decide that observation is the only way to learn to teach capably, let's look at what the method is and is not.

It is an opportunity to watch one teacher or a group of teachers teach one group of individuals in one environment. It is not in any way the last word on teaching. It is not intended that you copy the performance in your own classroom. Observation may give you insights into the solutions of knotty problems in your situation. You may learn to say, "It's time for all of us to pick up and clean up," instead of, "Who would like to help clean up this mess?" You may sense that a loud, strident voice encourages other loud, strident voices, and that a conversational tone can be heard as well, if everyone else uses it too. You may see for the first time the importance of looking at the persons you are talking with. Or you may start some mental rumination about your room arrangement or bulletin boards. If observing a master teacher encourages you to improve your teaching and look for new ways to do old things, it is worthwhile. But, if you watch expertise at work defensively, you are not ready for what the method has to offer.

- "We could never do that in our church."
- "You have so much room here."
- "We can't do that in Sunday clothes."
- "The children were on their best behavior."
- "You don't have to share your room."
- "Of course, this is an ideal setup."

Over and over in observation sessions we have heard these things said. One of the places referred to as an "ideal setup" was a drafty living room and kitchen in an old house. The kindergarten through second-grade children called it "headquarters" for some reason. The teacher was a stranger to them, and they advised her during the session that she had to turn the faucet marked "C" if she wanted hot water because both faucets had "C" on them.

She was told that they were to use the back door, because the front porch had been rained on so much it was rotting. And while they were seated on the floor conversing after a story, a child informed her that she would have to think up something for them to do in the kitchen or on the floor because they didn't have enough chairs for everyone. (The observers were using them.)

In another observation session, the regular teacher of the class was an observer. She had given the visiting teacher her capsule judgment of each student, and in summing up, added, "You'll have your hands full." The eighth-graders straggled in, boys on one side of the room, girls on the other. The man divided them in research teams of two people each. Then every team met with another "in committee" before bringing their findings to the "board." They worked hard for fifty minutes and then evaluated what they had done and how they had done it. One of the boys wrote, "College must be something like this."

Praise came spontaneously from the observers after the students had left, but the regular teacher turned to the person next to her and said, "They were on their best behavior." If they were, they hadn't come with that idea in mind.

Sometime you might have the opportunity to observe yourself teaching. Leaders at some events use videotape to encourage church school teachers to use their skills in the most efficient, most useful ways. Teachers volunteered to have their sessions videotaped and then watched themselves to learn more about their teaching. You also may have the opportunity to watch portions of videotaped sessions taught by master teachers featuring a single technique, such as how to phrase questions for lively discussions.

Master teachers can help in ways other than demonstrating their teaching skills. They can help you plan your units, arrange your teaching space, and find out more about techniques you want to try. If you feel up to it, you might ask a master teacher to visit your class as an observer.

As is true of any group of people, these teachers have their strong points and shortcomings. Some are adept at teaching a specific age group and inept at working with adults. Some cannot shoulder criticism and tend to defend themselves even when it is unnecessary. A long-retired woman who worked well with fifth- and sixth-graders told a group of observers after a session, "Don't ask me why I did this or that. I don't know."

One woman was asked why she used such horrible words as *stuff* and *junk*.

"What did I say?" she asked.

"Put your stuff away, and throw the scraps in our junk box," the critic repeated.

"Oh, I'm sorry," she said. "I am colloquial by nature. Next time I'll try to remember to say, 'Put your paraphernalia away and throw the scraps in our refuse container.'"

Personnel from your denomination's offices in charge of education in the churches can assist you in several ways.

Some of the events planned by area Christian education workers include people from denominational offices who demonstrate various methods and techniques not commonly used by most people attending. The most proficient ones try to teach their students the way they would hope these men and women would teach other adults. In an area meeting, the crowd is not representative of every church; some congregations seldom, if ever, send anyone. It is the responsibility of the group to share what they have learned with others, in their own congregation and elsewhere.

Denominational educators, like all of us, are mortal. Their standards of excellence and their abilities to achieve them are not all alike. They get tired, rushed, flustered, and cross, the way we all do. And some probably get that way quicker than others. One thing is almost generally true: they were employed previously in educational work and active in local churches.

Something else that is not as generally true but far more common than their students at these events realize is that they have had experience in several churches and know many more church situations than the rest of us because of their itinerations. They may not be any more perceptive about a situation or sympathetic toward you in a predicament than your next-door neighbor, but the church experience is behind them and around them if they are able to draw on it. They don't work in an ivory tower; they work in a lab.

Another way to find out specific information you can't get anywhere else is to write to your denominational offices to a specific person if you know a name. Ask where *you* can find the information, not for a hand-hewn list of the best VCR's for elementary children. The person may refer the letter to someone else who refers it to someone else, but you merit an answer for inquiring in the first place. Before you write, see if your area Christian education consultant can help you.

If you have a serious quarrel with factual material in curriculum courses, you are doing the editors a favor by writing to tell them. Editors trust writers and manuscript readers. They have to. They aren't all-wise in all things. Perhaps some of the misinformation is not too important in relation to the whole, but nonetheless, a mistake need not be reprinted or go uncorrected. Matters of geography, archaeology, biography, and the size of a sycamore tree in Palestine have come to editors' desks. Sometimes the correspondents are mistaken, but more often the editor is grateful for the specialist's knowledge. If you write protest letters to newspapers, you probably will write letters to curriculum course editors too. They get them now and then, but for every person protesting a viewpoint, there is one commending the same thing. It isn't logical; it's just so.

The pulse of the church is not felt so much by the volume of mail, because the mail doesn't come that fast or often.

The people who travel from place to place working with clusters of churches, local groups of teachers, and individuals using the curriculum materials are the ones who hear the whole band playing. Here we refer to them as teacher advocates or resource consultants. They are educators. In their reports to area and national offices and conversations with the people working there, they give as accurate a picture of how resources are being received, used, and misused as they are able. One essential characteristic that each of them learns eventually is to listen to criticism and complaints and then discuss them. They are far better acquainted with a variety of resources than almost anyone at the meetings. They have their opinions, peeves, and prejudices about the materials too. We all do.

INTERCHURCH CHRISTIAN EDUCATORS

Interdenominational councils in some areas may offer services in the field of Christian education and specifically teacher education. These services vary radically from place to place. The only way to find out is to ask what help is available. Councils are most helpful to the people who do not have area Christian educators to help them.

Directors and ministers of Christian education can be most helpful to you. Even if every church could afford a director of Christian education or a minister for that work, there would be nowhere near enough trained people to fill the vacancies. Most of these people, if not asked to excess, are willing and pleased to assist you or your whole teaching staff in pursuit of higher standards for education in the churches.

Of course, they vary in their abilities and interests. Don't expect them to be fountains of wisdom or even common knowledge. Find out what they do well, and ask the ones who can help you. They are hired by another church; don't take their services for granted. Their work with you is like walking the second mile after assuming the first was a healthy worker's limit.

Make appointments with them in advance of the time you want to see them, and state briefly what help you need. If you want to borrow something, assure the person that you will bring it back, then be sure you do. It is understandable, although annoying, to know that people in small churches can be resentful of the generosity of a larger one.

Two women from two different churches used to borrow books, videotapes and audiocassettes, additional curriculum resources, and advice from a large suburban church, taking great leisure to return items. Their attitudes were similar. They assumed that whatever they wanted was theirs for as long as they wanted it.

Finally the minister asked the D.C.E., "What are you going to do about it?"

"Nothing," she answered. "I want them to know that we will do whatever we can for them. Large-church Christians can't be all bad."

You don't have to be grateful, but be kind. And if you can't be kind, be pleasant.

Informal interchurch educational groups, sometimes formed to last only four or five weeks and meeting one evening a week, pool some of the finest talent in the community. Not only do nuns, deaconesses, ministers, and priests contribute to such a school, but day school teachers, professors, counselors, and psychologists may also be available for teaching. If you hear of an interchurch educational enterprise, try it out. They have a great deal to offer, and although there is surely opportunity for improvement in them, they need your support. You are the reason they exist.

EVENTS YOU MIGHT CONSIDER WORTHWHILE

Many services are offered to church school teachers at educational meetings, study groups, and schools. It stands to reason that what your church offers you is probably closer to what you need, but some churches offer very little besides free curriculum resources and a handshake at the door. We call all of these learning opportunities "events," hoping that in them something happens. That is what an event is—something that happens. The variations from place to place approach infinity in number, but there are only a few basic patterns.

One-day events are particularly common in urban centers where public transportation gets you where you want to go and Saturdays are relatively free. These one-day events can be most helpful to new teachers because there is a limit to how much anyone can retain before experience confirms, "This is worth remembering."

There were three people, a man and two women, in a corridor of a church building during a coffee break at a one-day event advertised as lecture, panel, and free-for-all. The lecture was over.

"Oh, I learned all that in college," one woman said, "It's just words, words, words."

"Well," the man said thoughtfully, "I *heard* it too, but I never *learned* it."

"I didn't go to college," the other woman broke in, "and it's welcome news to me."

For her the day was an event.

One-day events are nourishment, but not whole meals. Maybe a snack is all you need.

Resident leadership schools for two days to a week are attended by only a few of the many teachers in the churches. They are held largely in the summer and generally have provision for childcare. They necessitate your being away from home, and for that reason, most of the families are taking vacation time to be at the school.

In the good schools, courses are as worthwhile as college courses. The value of the school cannot be measured by the courses though. Meeting experts and amateurs informally is an education in itself.

Two incidents following an Ohio resident school show the effect associations at the school have on both teachers and students.

A woman was reading her fall units and discussing plans with a friend. "Whoever wrote this material can surely talk to people. It's almost as if that woman who taught my class at leadership school from downstate were talking to me." She was. She had written the units.

A man was watching television one evening when the news revealed an important discovery in medicine in Cleveland. Suddenly his wife shouted from another room: "Ira! I taught his wife at leadership school!"

Resident schools are for a fortunate minority. It is comforting to know that some of our fellow teachers are not content to buzz lampposts when there are stars they can reach with more effort.

Commuter schools are an urban invention. Some cities offer them at night. When observation is part of the schools, the children are tired, and though they may try valiantly to be normal for your benefit, it isn't easy.

If you have an opportunity to go to a commuter school, you won't regret it. It is very likely that the people working there are closer to your situation that those in a resident school. It is not always true that the teachers in resident schools are better educated and more experienced than those in commuter schools. It is more likely, though, that you will find fledgling instructors in a commuter school, and you seldom do at a resident school. They have to cut their teeth on something.

Children in a commuter observation class are from

the neighborhood. Sometimes the cultural differences noted in the children from a city church and those from a suburban one help both city and suburban teachers better understand the children they teach.

For example, a kindergarten class in a Chicago school was discussing pets.

"Who has a pet in his or her house? Anyone?" the teacher asked the cliff dwellers. They all raised their hands.

"Do you suppose you could bring them Friday for our parade?" They could. "Remember that means go to bed tonight, get up, go to bed the next night, and then it's Friday."

They remembered. On Friday twelve stuffed animals came to church. Apartment pets. The suburban observers were astonished. The city observers were amused but not surprised.

Whereever you watch a teacher at work, you can learn something you didn't know before.

PLACES TO KNOW ABOUT

There are addresses you should know if you are in a position to suggest the ordering of items or procuring of human resources for teacher education. Write the names and addresses underneath the headings below. Each event you go to will offer you more resources for the list.

PEOPLE

Area Christian Educator
Consultant for Curriculum Resources
Director or Minister of Education
Librarian

Minister
Church School Superintendent
Other Teachers
Substitutes
Someone I Met at a Meeting

WHERE TO FIND OUT ABOUT

Art Prints from Museum
Bookstore Catalogs
Computer Network
Making Nursery and Kindergarten Furniture
Videotapes for Class Use
New Books and Tapes for My Use
Teacher Education

Add more information on the inside back cover. That is one of the reasons we have it.

CHAPTER 6
Beginning Is the Hardest

With all the help you get from materials, equipment, and other people, ultimately it is your mind that goes to work, your energy that is dispensed, and your eyes that do the reading and observing. Whether you are to teach in a cubicle as the only adult with your pupils or in the dining room with two teachers, you are responsible for your own performance.

Many suggestions of methods and techniques will be new to you, old as they are. Day school teachers have registered surprise for years at the varied techniques used by proficient volunteers in the church school. Two supervisory employees of school systems in large cities in the Midwest were envying the naiveté, they called it, of church school teachers in a skills workshop they were helping to lead.

The art supervisor said, "They'll try anything. It doesn't seem to occur to them that they can't!" He went on to say that his experienced public school teachers, with their large classes and complex problems in keeping order, were happy to have him do something with their classes but were afraid to go it alone with even simple, untried techniques. He applauded our small classes and our determination to accomplish something, but most of all our willingness to vary our teaching techniques and our excitement at learning new ones.

The elementary supervisor's comment was telling indeed. She said, "You expect to get more variety and substance into less than an hour than we do all day. Don't ever go to all day. You'll start wasting time."

Our naiveté is a great gift, and we must not lose it by developing fear. Others have done well at what you are asked to do.

Techniques in art, music, drama, storytelling, and discussion are only ways to get things done. You have an objective or a reason for what you are doing. Techniques are ways to get you to the point where you can reread the objective and say, "We did that."

Some units lend themselves to one set of techniques better than to another. For instance, with the whole story of Abraham's moving with his wife, nephew, and tribe from Haran to Ur and subsequently to Canaan, informal dramatization is a natural technique. In any dramatic endeavor, movement takes place. Coupled with an eagerness for dramatization in six- to ten-year-olds, the technique fits the subject matter and the children. The only reason left for not dramatizing the event is the teacher who doesn't know how.

Your materials tell you how in varying degrees. Sometimes for lack of space or effort, they will say, "Dramatize the story." That can mean anything from an operetta to a well-told story with gestures. Other times, and often, general instructions for informal dramatization are given.

The problem that usually exists is small in terms of its solution, and larger than life if no solution is given. It is simply, "How do I get started?"

This initial question is an issue in most of the techniques we use in teaching. Done well, many of our superficial problems with order and discipline vanish. Done poorly, havoc reigns.

In art, crafts, music, drama, and just plain listening, once you begin in a wholesome, knowledgeable manner, your students carry the ball. We need to be starters. The technique is a windup toy, and we hold the key. Releasing it at the right time is crucial. It is the students who play with it. Occasionally, we hear that a teacher's job is to remove himself or herself from learners. This is *never* true. We may not be the prime movers. Content and the students themselves may run the show. But a teacher is always there with eyes, mind, and judgment central to whatever goes on in the room.

CONVERSATION AND DISCUSSION

Everyone who teaches can talk. Most of us talk too much. Both conversation and discussion mean that we listen while someone else talks. With young children, your easy, firm manner as you speak with them will probably bring forth their best thoughts. Unless they have been schooled by other adults to give pat answers, they will tell the truth. This can be devastating as well as refreshing.

A neophyte teacher asked a group of five-year-olds in Wisconsin one snowy Sunday morning, "Who makes it snow?" Before any of the believers in the Great Snowmaker in the Sky could answer, a wistful, blond, Scandanavian boy answered, "There's an old man in Medicine Hat, Canada, who makes the weather."

"Oh, I read that story when I was a child, Eric!" the teacher told him. "I had almost forgotten about that."

"My father can make it snow," the daughter of a skier volunteered. "He said this morning that if it hadn't snowed, he was going up there to *make* it snow."

"I think it just snows," one solitary oyster commented from the edge of the group. "It's winter, and it snows."

The young teacher was visibly amused. Her smile betrayed her light heart to the other teachers. She said: "I was going to tell you who makes snow, but you have so many ideas that I haven't thought of. You ask your family when you get home. See what you can find out."

The next Sunday she was greeted by Eric with, "Miss Lund, the weatherman tells us what the weather will be. If it's cold and cloudy up in the sky, it will snow. And God makes everything go."

Miss Lund's discussion yielded far more satisfactory results than her perfunctory question deserved.

With older children and young people, it is possible to start a discussion and have interaction within the group. It is truly a round table discussion, not an answer-the-teacher game. To encourage the kind of talking it takes, remove yourself from the usual position of teacher.

A group of senior highs had just seen a video conjecturing about a solemn year 2030. The teacher sat with the youth, asked a few questions, received a few questions, and then said: "Don't ask me. I'll by 69 years old, and you will be the pacesetters, lawmakers, and commentators of the current situation. It's your world."

When content as well as physical arrangement phase out the teacher as authority, you are well on your way to genuine discussion.

Pat answers are with us always. Someone is sure to think the teacher has an answer in mind and is willing to guess what it is. The only time you should have an answer in mind is when there is only one answer to the question.

- What was Peter's former name?
- What significant contributions did Peter make to the Christian faith?

Do you see the difference between the questions? Do you see which one calls for discussion?

Dealing with pat answers is part of beginning on the right foot in teaching. Those persons who give them need to think beyond the easy answer to other more searching responses. If they want only to please you, ask them more questions of the kind that will make them think more deeply. If they are afraid to think, perhaps they need to listen to others articulating their beliefs.

Conversation and discussion go on at every age level after children speak in sentences. It is up to us to foster honest responses even in the three-year-olds' conversations.

In the meeting room of one group of three-year-olds, there was a small basket on a folding table just inside the door where parents left a pittance called an "offering." No attention was called to it, money meaning little to a three-year-old. One day a child came in with his father. The man went through his pockets frantically. The teacher, greeting them, said to the father, "Don't worry, Andy, we'll take care of him without the price of admission."

The child took hold of his father's hand. "Daddy, you don't have to have a ticket to get in here, you know."

A competent teacher says of his manner with eighth-graders, "We don't discuss anything. The class visits." Perhaps what we need is more visiting and less structured discussion.

MUSIC

Interlaced into every unit of preschool and elementary teaching is a multitude of activities involving music. Children sing, write tunes, make up words to old tunes, shake rhythm instruments, and dance. For the unmusical teacher, this field is a mystery. But if you ignore it, you are depriving your group of a dimension of education they need. The purpose of all musical activities in the church school is to prepare the learners for intelligent participation in corporate worship.

Music belongs to the church.

With all the activities suggested, what you want most of all is to have a singing church school. Any activity that helps a child sing is worth your while. Any activity that teaches a child he or she cannot sing is worth your scorn.

A woman who has worked with preschool children for many years tells of her inability to sing. The children sang off key and with no tune, but they sang. She taught them the words. Finally, she sat down at the piano, played a middle C, and sang until her voice found it. She disciplined herself until she could sing on key. Today she is able to sight-read and sing without a piano.

Your first hurdle with music is to sing. That much you can practice at home. If you can read music, you are ahead. Here is why. Look at the key signature and determine "do." Then look at the space between the first note and the next. Let's say it's from "do" to "fa." The song then begins like "Auld Lang Syne." Spaces between notes, or intervals, can be calculated by intervals in well-known songs. If you hit minor or modal tunes, you may be in trouble, but this is a good start.

A group of fifth-graders were taught to sightsing in this way. They made remarkable progress. When one child made a musical error, another said, "That's 'Day Is Done,' John, not 'I Pledge.'" They could sightsing a whole song with their interval code.

If you are past these rudimentary skills, you can get on to composing music and words. The reasons we make up music to words of Scripture is to set apart the words for thinking. Two sixth-graders worked with 1 Peter 2:10a. At first they gave it the tune to "Onward, Christian Soldiers," but were dissatisfied until they came up with an original melody. It will never make music history, but the process they went through is noteworthy. They put the first line all on one tone, because "nothing was happening." It went, "Once you were no people..." Then they repeated the second line twice, taking it up and down and all around before ending it. "But now you are God's people" was good news. Here the teacher did nothing more than consent to the writing of the song and listen to the two children tell how it was written after they had finished.

In some churches, music is a special service, done by professional leadership. Here the end is the same—a singing church school. Listen and participate with the children. There is so much you can learn to improve your teaching. All of us can sing; we just don't all sing well.

STORYTELLING

Being able to spin a tale is invaluable with young children, and even worthwhile with adults. Books, articles, and pamphlets have been written on how to tell a story. They offer advice such as stand in front of a mirror, use body movement, know your story well, look at your audience, and forget that you're scared. After a while, presumably, all of this works toward good storytelling.

At the beginning, only you know what kind of a storyteller you are. If it comes easily, fine. If you are self-conscious, look at the ceiling when you forget, or lunge for the printed word, you aren't ready for *telling* a story yet. Try reading it well first. Reading aloud is an accepted legacy an older generation gives the young.

A middle-aged woman in a very small town in Missouri said that she had learned the value of reading to children when an older woman's Bible stories were recorded and copied for use in her church school. She had grown up hearing the woman tell the stories, and when she taught, she read them as the woman had told them. One of them for early elementary children starts, "Once upon a time, oh, let me see, before there were cars and way before your grandfather was a boy, there lived a man and a woman who wanted to have a little boy of their very own." The story of Samuel from boy to man follows.

There are those linguists who say there is no difference between oral and written language. They would have to admit that some written language begs to be read aloud.

Before you meet your class with a story, read it aloud at home. Become familiar with your voice and what it can do. Don't be afraid to use the versatile equipment you've been given, not only to be understood but to be believed. You aren't telling the adventures of Sinbad the Sailor.

A college girl, fulfilling a requirement for a child development course, was teaching a church school class of third-graders. She was like one of those people the art supervisor mentioned earlier: she didn't know she couldn't, and somehow managed to do almost anything she was asked to do. She was reading a story of Nehemiah returning to Jerusalem and viewing his ruined city. She departed from the printed word as the story became part of her.

"Look at the wall! It is ruined!" she cried. "Well, I'll have to fix it." she stopped. "But I can't do it all by myself. *What* will I do?"

The children, accustomed to dramatic play on a truer-than-life basis, responded.

"I'm a carpenter. I'll bring a hammer."

"I'll pile up the bricks. O.K.?"

"I'll bring some drinking water."

The young teacher's fieldwork supervisor's comment was one we should remember on days when the unexpected best happens to us in response to our mediocre efforts: "This can only happen when you forget yourself."

No one asks you to forget *yourself*, really. Forgetting unwarranted fears, self-consciousness, and debilitating inhibitions is remembering and hanging on to the best that you are. Storytelling takes so little time. Don't let it interrupt your lifespan. Let it enrich it instead.

DRAMA

Dramatic activity is as simple as girls and boys being a semblance of a family at a housekeeping center or as complicated as a group of senior highs and adults putting on a production of *Waiting for Godot*. Most of the dramatic skills that church school teachers seek are between those two extremes. It's what we call "informal drama" that most of us do. Your teaching plans and a few good books listed in your materials explain the intricacies of costumes and varieties of performance.

At first, don't worry about costumes, and don't even worry about twenty-seven ways to do fourteen types of drama. Just stick to what is suggested. And then use your common sense as you've never used it before. Think through the whole activity.

It is true that children love to dramatize and they are spontaneous. The latter, if the teacher is unprepared, gets in the way of the former.

In a church in the High Sierras, an after-school group was meeting on a Wednesday afternoon. It was a red-letter day because someone from denominational offices was coming to visit. The teachers prepared the session to the second. Everything suggested in the plans would be used. They had never dramatized before, but this time they would. Silas and Paul were in prison, singing hymns, and the jailers were amazed. The costumes were greedily acquired. The props were given out after the first, unfortunate question: "Who would like to be a guard and have a spear?" Such a war you never saw! If it had not been for otherwise competent teaching, the armed conflict would have ended with at least one bloody nose. No mention of pointed, wooden spears was given in the printed session plan. That was the outgrowth of exuberant inexperience in one area of teaching. The teachers were wise in giving out bit parts first. But swords as rewards to the forgotten extras? No.

Though some teachers find it easy, many well-seasoned dramatists of the informal variety say it as far from simple to allow the freedom that spontaneous drama demands.

Recently, some refreshing informal dramatic activity has taken place. Children have been told that the squares and lengths of cloth, cords and sashes, the veils and sandals are there to use in costume-making. A few second-graders one morning made costumes from scraps, even attaching old brooches to gathering points, while going about their usual activities rather than preferring dramatic play. The teacher, in the midst of the story said, "Jacob had two wives." Planning to go further with her story, she was interrupted by a costumed child who said, "Me and her."

She said, "Oh, which of you is Leah, and which is Rachel?"

"I'm Leah, because I'm the oldest."

"And I'm Rachel, because I'm little and pretty." Leah seemed to accept the assessment as part of living.

It's hard to say what the first steps in drama are, except to stress an open door to the spontaneous and to warn against the temptation to contrive for effect. Spontaneous drama is elusive, engaging, and deeply humorous.

A few years ago a group of inner-city middle-schoolers were contemporizing an early-church scene in which rumors of peculiar practices were reported against the Christians. The teacher recorded it for use in area teacher education events.

Nurse:	Hello, Mrs. Edwards
Mrs. E:	Nurse, where is my baby?
Nurse:	Your baby?
Mrs. E:	Yes, where did you ditch my baby?
Nurse:	I heard you Christians ate babies...
Mrs. E:	You're kidding! Bring him back!
Nurse:	He's still here. I wouldn't hurt a baby. I'm not a Christian!

(Then the heart-rending conversion took place.)

Nurse:	I want to become a Christian!
Mrs. E:	Why?
Nurse:	Because you love people!
Mrs. E:	You thought I didn't love my baby!
Nurse:	I was wrong! I was wrong! I wanted your baby! Now I know . . . . . .
Teacher:	Let's think this scene through again. It's a bit lachrymose, and there's a dictionary for those who don't know what that means.

Young teenagers are likely to get ahead of themselves. The teacher who called them back with the dictionary word had a fairly penetrating conversation with them. At their age, that is a good reason for drama.

Successful informal drama takes place on the spot. It isn't predictable. You don't need realistic props at first, with any age person. And forget about spears for the jailers.

ARTS AND CRAFTS

Your curriculum materials will lead you step by step in almost any large-scale project. They may not tell you how long it will take or what parts of the project can be abbreviated. For example, any number of assorted puppet stages are better off made at home, to be used with puppets made in class. One good reason for making your stage beforehand is that a knife, a pasteboard box, and a group of children are a potentially dangerous combination, no matter how careful the teacher intends to be. Another reason is that you're taking a great deal of time to do something that has little or no educational value in the church. (If someone tells you that children grow in community doing a whole project together, find one not requiring a knife.)

There are ways to shorten the birth of a puppet too. If you are using papier-maché for the head, you don't have to spend the first session tearing up paper and soaking it according to your recipe. That can be done ahead of time. One of the grossest misuses of church school time took place over an entire semester in a sixth-grade class. They made puppets. On the second Sunday of June, when the church corridors and walls resembled a sidewalk art show, that sixth-grade class had nothing to show. They were putting hair on the puppets they had never had an opportunity to use. The purpose of making puppets in a church school class is to use them there in dramatization.

There is a reason or an objective behind each project. Keep that reason or objective in mind.

Sometimes a project doesn't catch on with the group. It may be that the children have already done that kind of craft too often, but usually it is not the process but the reason for doing it that escapes them. It is true that third-graders get fairly tired of the color-the-picture routine, but it is not crayons they dislike—it's the pictures. As one boy put it, "You'd think a kid who's eight years old could draw his own pictures." The teacher turned the patterned sheet over. "Here," she said, "use this." If you detect a lack of interest in pursuing a major project, think of your reason for doing it and see if you can terminate the project more quickly than planned without losing the point of it in the first place. You don't want half-finished art projects around. They have a way of teaching negatively.

With older children and young people, you should be able to decide together what you want to accomplish and why. You needn't inflict arts and crafts on them for the mere reason that variety in teaching is desirable. Some young people thoroughly enjoy learning by using their hands and minds. Some do not. It is not your purpose in teaching in the church to insist on skill development in arts and crafts. Our job is to use what they have used elsewhere to satisfy the objectives of education in the church.

More and more, to the delight of children, teachers

have found in drawing, painting, freehand tearing and cutting, and use of textured materials valuable ways of expressing artistically what was learned through story or Scripture study.

There are a few things you need to know to begin working with these art materials. They can set you free, for instance, to observe what misconceptions still need to be cleared up. When a fourth-grade child draws a picture of the Holy Ghost, your work is just beginning.

To avoid small catastrophes in elementary classrooms, begin with a few standards.

You can cover a section of the floor with plastic before paper and paints are in evidence. Ask for volunteers for painting, and limit the number to the space you have and the number of aprons or shirts you have. Ask the children to plan the painting in their minds first, even if it is part of a cooperative project such as a mural. Then put the paints in the center of the group that is painting so that no one has to reach too far, drip on someone else's paper, or spill. Pick up the paints as soon as the children are finished.

In cooperative projects, using textures, torn paper, or freehand drawing and cutting, plan the whole picture before pasting. Children don't like to look at a poster they spoiled, especially when classmates are ready to remind them of it each time they see it too. Keep some wet sponges around the pasting area for both people and surfaces.

Warn busy groups five minutes before you must abandon the projects. It takes a few minutes to terminate even before cleaning-up time comes.

Use the completed art projects for review in future

sessions. They are part of your equipment. And if you're particularly proud of what the whole group has done, have an exhibit for others in the church. It's one more opportunity for the boys and girls to give reasons for their projects.

LISTENING

With all the skills you might develop by being courageous enough to try anything twice, listening is the only skill you cannot do without.

- Listen when a child talks to you at the door.
- Listen when children talk to one another as they work.
- Listen when a young person says, "Why do we have to?"
- Listen to the questions you ask. Would you have liked to answer them? Did they make you think?
- Listen to your voice. So few of us do.

LOOKING AROUND YOU

A four-year-old boy told his mother that his teacher was the tallest person in the world. When she questioned the claim, he said, "Her eyes can never find me. They're way up high."

We who talk about observing behavior sometimes forget to just plain look at those we teach.

Children, because they are not yet our height, are more aware than adults of not being seen, hence, to them, not being thought of. The younger the child, the harder it is to face being ignored in a group. Even if a boy comes from a family of eight, he is still the only one his size at home. Being in a group of strangers all near his own size is irregular enough, but when the adult's eyes can never find the child, he is alone indeed.

Looking around you is a good place to begin.

THINKING ON THE SPOT

A skill that develops with familiarity, if one is aware of it, is being able to reflect on and assess actions of individuals and the temperament of the group. It is mentioned here only so that you won't immediately blame yourself for the inevitable days when things could have gone a lot better than they did. Many factors are at work in every classroom. Besides each pupil's experiences at home and in the neighborhood, changes in weather, no change in weather, stale air in the room, not enough light, a fire engine going by, or a loud noise in the hallway can affect a group.

Upon reflection you may find there are ways to counteract group mood. That is one reason for learning to think on the spot. You can correct an uncomfortable group atmosphere before it becomes obvious to the pupils.

We all begin somewhere as we learn to teach others. We expect to have weaknesses to work on and surely, certain strengths.

Nevertheless, no one has grown to adulthood as a beginner. We couldn't possibly have muddled through life without picking up a good bit that is worth passing on to the young.

CHAPTER 7
Go with God

Now you have your books. Stuff them in a backpack, throw them over your shoulder, and go with God. You have the support of so many people that your fear, enthusiasm, or indifference cannot help being affected. The magicians, Santa Clauses, coaches, families, best friends, day school teachers, second lieutenants, and ordinary teachers are with you. We want you to do well. You have a story to tell in as many ways as you know how: Christ came that we might know God and be friends with one another. Try that much first.

Relax and Laugh

You have a great many books, magazines, and resources for your use. Look through them and see where you are supposed to be going. Then relax. Take a unit at a time. Teach a session at a time, a minute at a time.

There is the school of thought that teaches that we must never waste a moment of educational time. Most of the people who espouse that theory are so busy watching the clock and their notes that they fail to see what effect their efforts have on their students. Know that time wasted never comes back, but realize that time enjoyed in laughter shared is never wasted. Love and laughter are akin, and when Christians stop seeing the humor in the conventional, they stop loving in that sphere. That is serious because the conventional is the sphere in which most of us operate.

Some of the favorite stories of church school teachers are taken from sessions with serious intent. Their laughter *with* the children was a means of teaching them and a very effective way of keeping teachers humble.

1. The first-grade children in one class were talking together about how to treat visitors, since the parents were invited the next week.

"You're nice to them."

"No, you treat them the way you do any old people. You're *careful* with them."

"Careful?" the teacher repeated.

"Yes. They worry if we jump around and yell."

Just then the minister walked through in his robe and stole, looking grand. He was not quite forty.

"Hello, Old-timer," a smiling, well-intentioned six-year-old greeted him.

2. A teacher of five-year-olds decided on Sunday, December 26, to talk about Christmas.

"What happened on Christmas? Why do we talk about it, sing about it, and remember it? Who knows?" the teacher prodded.

"Oh, I know, Mrs. Stubbs," a quavering voice volunteered, "That was the day our train blew up."

3. A teacher of third-graders decided to serve raisins in the newly built facsimile of a Palestinian home. When she opened the raisins in front of the class, one box had dark ones and the other box, light. As they fell into the dishes, an astute eight-year-old African American boy laughed: "Oh-oh! Integrated raisins."

4. A seventh-grade boy told about being in a class where the teacher always referred to books of the Bible by saying, "Take Isaiah. Take Mark." One morning the teacher said, "Take Ruth and Esther." Ruth Dingle said, "You can take Esther, but I want to stay."

This is how the teachers answered each of the incidents given. You may have better ideas, but you have time to reflect on your responses; they didn't.

1. The minister laughed. The teacher said, "Mr. Wilson, we are talking about how to treat visitors because their parents are coming next Sunday."

Mr. Wilson looked approvingly at the children. With a serious countenance he said, "Give them chairs to sit on. They aren't as young as you are."

The children arranged the chairs before they left.

2. Mrs. Stubbs laughed. She was a great-grandmother. Children like to see their grandmothers laugh.

"I didn't mean last Christmas—yesterday. I meant the first Christmas. Why do we have Christmas?"

"Oh," another child said. "You mean Jesus. That's easy. The baby king. I know him."

3. The teacher laughed because the child laughed. Wit needs an audience in order to thrive.

4. The teacher, of dry wit and intelligence known to all, said, "I said, 'Take Ruth.' Now *she* was a book, Miss Dingle." Everyone laughed at "taking Ruth" along with Esther. Good teachers of seventh-graders learn to adjust to their early adolescent brands of humor and to remunerate in kind.

THE INDIVIDUALS IN YOUR GROUP

As you begin teaching, you are bound to learn more about the peculiar combination of personalities you have in your class. It is easy to play what one lawyer, a senior high teacher, calls the "spook game." He refers to the practice of some "corridor psychologists" who try to discover hidden motives in those students giving us trouble, those who don't get along with others, and those who rarely like themselves. Psychologists and psychiatrists, particularly, are far more reluctant than the armchair analysts to diagnose with such limited evidence as we might have, if indeed it is evidence at all. The lawyer called such diagnoses invasions of privacy.

Our job is to be teachers and to teach we need to be sensitive to situations that encourage our students to learn and to be aware of what keeps them from learning. That is hard enough for most of us, without trying unsuccessfully to examine egos we cannot see.

A teacher of kindergarten with many years experience in giving psychological tests to young children had a difficult time maintaining order in a church school. She said she had never seen children who were so lacking in respect for authority.

She was asked: "Who are the ringleaders? Who are the followers? What do they have to do when they first arrive? What do you do to move the group smoothly from one activity to another? What attitudes toward learning and just being at church do the individual children have?"

She answered the questions most inadequately, and as she talked, it was apparent that she saw individuals and looked at their performance in a group, but that she seldom looked at the group as a whole. Her comments about the children, individually, had little relationship to her general indictment concerning resistance to authority. They sounded as if she had tried to step inside the back of each head directly behind the eyeballs and look at the world through each individual's eyes.

The children were not resistant to authority. They simply didn't have any authority to resist. Not being accustomed to groups of children, the teacher was not able to observe more than one at a time, and for that reason could not anticipate what the group would do or even what an individual was doing to the group. She was not aware that smooth transitions are necessary to move a whole group from an active time to a relatively quiet time. She hadn't thought of the effect children have on other children, only the effect they have on one child at a time. She never realized after many improvements in her teaching that the group needed active and quiet times so that they would go home refreshed rather than exhausted. Groups have to breathe, just as a person must. There is a time to take in and a time to give out.

The teacher's control of a group is for the welfare of every person in the group. Of course we observe individuals, relate to them, and watch them as they learn. That is teaching, to put it in a word. And that is precisely why we can never tell another person how to be a good teacher all the time.

Every thumbnail sketch and every anecdote in this book involving interpersonal relationships tells us only what the chemistry was in one situation and how two or more people who were unlike any other people in the world known to human existence reacted, learned, or resisted change.

Scenes from real life help us *anticipate* (that is an important activity and a word that means to get ready and set *before* you go) our own actions in the multitude of *experiences* (and that word means all that happens to us whether significant or trivial) that occur while teaching and knowing other mortals.

"Experience" itself means living in a job—or one after another—long enough to make some accurate generalizations from many specifics. In the absence of our own specifics, as novices, we use those belonging to others. That kind of lending most veteran teachers approve of and enjoy. They remember how little they knew at the beginning. Those who don't remember, understandably, have little to share that can help the inexperienced.

One woman said that she used to tell her fellow teachers that she never had problems with discipline until "one day, one month, one year, I had them aplenty.

I was sixty-eight years old, and I'm sure it was the class and not me, but those women I taught with welcomed me into a society of humility and concern for those boys and girls that this conceited old lady never knew existed. It was a minor conversion—a pentecost with a small 'p.' The older I get the more I understand God's mercy. God loves the foolish, the children, and those who think they can go it alone every bit as much the faithful. I've told the story of the prodigal son year after year. He was always the other fellow to me, and now he is this one, here, writing the letter."

She is ready now to help the uninitiated. Only those who remember their Achilles' heels can be supportive teachers of teachers. Achilles' heels are:

- thinking you are exempt
- deciding whatever it is doesn't apply to you
- believing it couldn't happen to you

Once you are hit, you know what to bandage and let heal. The best way to cure the heel is to show it and tell the story of how you were shot down.

One more word should be uttered about law and order before we discuss term of office. Trouble or no trouble, everyone worries about "keeping school." Some naturally, or seemingly so, keep it better than others. You may think you have jumped through the final ring of fire for church school teachers; be prepared for "the fire next time" and help those who are afraid to try.

Human beings are still riddles to human beings. Sometimes we are riddles to ourselves. Jesus said, "In everything do to others as you would have them do to you" (Matthew 7:12 NRSV). Does it sound simple? Try it and see. A distinguished, hard-working train of souls goes before you. If you pass us on the tracks and your caboose has a hitch, come back and take us along. We have the little engine that couldn't but for the grace of God.

TERM OF SERVICE

Remember that you don't have to teach for the rest of your life unless you want to do it. Duty is not the best reason to accept the job of teaching in the church. Gratitude is.

The benediction "Go with God" doesn't specify a set of rules for devotional behavior. It simply acknowledges that you belong to God, and your acceptance of a fact that is already true is the beginning of faith. Again and again people ask, "What is unique about being a Christian? Many people do good to others. Many teach their traditions to the young and uninitiated."

It is this. We admit our gross imperfection and live with it. We work hard at doing good to others and teaching the young and the sojourners within our gates. But our unique quality is our unique Jesus. In the words of the spiritual, "No man works like him." Only the Son of God was without sin in our world, for only God is perfect.

A woman who has served the church and the world for at least twenty-five years tells of a Sunday morning when her teenage daughter approached her in bed at 9:30.

"Mother, why aren't you getting ready for church?" she asked.

"Oh, Laura, I've had an upset stomach since 2:30 this morning. I feel terrible."

114

"Oh, come on, Mother!" Laura cheered. "Nobody's perfect."

That's the way it is with us. Welcome to the club!

Appendix

Chapter 1

Innovation

Some very useful objects from common life are also handy to have in your classroom, especially as you begin to get acquainted with your group. The objects are on the left. Their uses are scrambled on the right. How innovative are you?

1.____A ball of clay

a. For book covers, collages, place mats, and walls

2.____Detergent

b. For modeling miniatures for a pictorial table map

3.____Wallpaper cleaner

c. For you and your substitute to identify names and faces

4.____Wallpaper

d. For a crying three-year-old or a nervous teacher

5.____Chewing gum

e. To put in poster paint so that the brushes come out clean when rinsed in water

6.____A list of your
pupils with snapshots of
them

f. For clay when the ner-
vous teacher has worn
out the supply

7.____A first-aid kit,
telephone numbers of
your pupils' parents,
and an agreed upon
pattern of exit when
the fire alarm rings

g. For the unforeseen

It doesn't matter too much how you answered the first six. They were to show you, by contrast, the importance of the seventh. We are notoriously careless about safety precautions in the church. A serious mishap takes only a fraction of a second, and there are 3,600 seconds in an hour at church. The correct answer is "g."

CHAPTER 2

WATCH YOUR LANGUAGE

Every discipline using words to justify its existence has special favorites that have taken on heavier loads than they can carry. Most of them you can translate, eventually, and when you do, you are a full-fledged member of the club. Then you have two choices: to use the words any way you want or to avoid them completely.

The first statement is a definition in our lingo; the second is a paraphrase in the English language.

Analyze

1. To examine cooperatively through inductive processes, arriving at no consensus, but striving for an expression of group satisfaction that learning has taken place.

2. To take apart and look at.

Synthesize

1. Upon gathering data and examining findings, to combine such learnings to comprise a whole.

2. To put together what you tore apart and hope that you learned something.

Behavioral Objective

1. An aim in the teaching-learning process requiring concrete, specific action to determine to the satisfaction of all that learning has taken place.

2. If you are given 100 words to learn to spell, and you write them all correctly, you know how to spell 100 words.

Motivation

1. Erroneously and often used as a synonym for manipulation. Correctly, it is that quality within us that inspires us to act in a learning situation to benefit ourselves because we want to learn.

2. A strong enough desire to know something so that we are willing to work at it.

Creativity

1. A gift for being able to make something from nothing, to think up new ways of doing old things, to discover new things and do them in new ways, to make the homely pretty, to have a flair.

2. A word meaning almost anything concerned with what one person can do that another cannot.

Now try doing your own glossary.

Learning experiences
    1.
    2.

Gathering of data
    1.
    2.

Evaluating the process
    1.
    2.

Your own verbal discovery
    1.
    2.

This was an exercise, not an exhaustive listing of educational terms. When you meet one, do the exercise.

CHAPTER 3

WALLS

A director of Christian education who found humor more persuasive than printed directives used to post "anonymous" poetry on the teachers' bulletin board when something was too important to overlook but not of major significance. When she became a professor, she disclosed herself as poet so that any poetry-writing student might use the same technique.

This Is What Some of Them Said
    Walls have ears, people say? I do not know.
    They have voices to speak. This is truly so.
    You can hear them speak just any day,
    For every wall has something to say,

And this is what some of them said:

CLASSROOM NO. 1

These walls were painted long ago.
Grandfather remembers. You could not know,
For the paint is covered with twelve years' cloak
Of summer's dust and winter's smoke. . .
They have said to the children, "You need not care
For the house of God, you need not share
For it time or money. Perhaps it's a duty
To clean your homes and give them beauty,
But the church? Forget it. The big folks do!
So you'd better just forget it too!"
What a *naughty* thing to tell them!

CLASSROOM NO. 2

These walls were clean as clean could be.
They said, "That's the way all walls should be."
That was all they said. What they said was good.
They said it well. It was understood.
But they said no more, for these walls were bare.
No pictures upon them called to prayer.
No artists were asked to help them speak
Of Beauty and Truth. All clean and bleak—
They had so *little* to say!

CLASSROOM NO. 3

"When I was a child, I spoke as a child,
And I understood as a little child."
These walls talked to children as though
they were grown,
Of the parable where the seed is sown,
In a fourfold picture—"A River of Life,"
The portrait of someone's sainted wife,

120

A photograph framed to commemorate
The Official Board of Nineteen Eight—
A satin red-and-golden script
Proclaiming a baseball championship—
These things had a message for those who
hung them;
There was not one childlike thing among them.
It was all *Greek* to the children.

CLASSROOM NO. 4

These walls spoke a language the children knew,
But nobody listened, as neither would you.
Nobody cared. When folks chatter and chatter,
We are likely to think, "What they say does not
matter!"
(Of course, if you hang all the pictures you get,
it saves you buying a cabinet.)
The primary set made a frieze round the wall.
It told all the stories from spring until fall
Until winter and then till spring again:
Of Daniel in the lions' den,
Of cherry gardens in Japan,
Elijah's faithless serving man,
Of children giving kitty drink,
Of springtime flowers blue and pink,
A sister with her little brother
In "Going to the Store for Mother,"
The shepherds in their glad surprise,
Some bees and ants and butterflies,
And so forth and et cetera.
Too bad they *chattered* so.

These sunny walls, in quiet voice
Through pictures of a thoughtful choice,
Spoke of the Christ-child and his mother,
Said "Be ye kind one to another,"
"Theirs is the kingdom, let them come,"
Just that. And on the burlap some
Few pictures chosen for the day
One thing harmoniously to say
In accents worthy of the place.
These walls helped children grow in grace.
They spoke with *authority!*

—Hulda Niebuhr

CHAPTER 4

BATS IN THE BELFRY

Once upon a time in the state just east of Oregon and west of Idaho, there lived a man who agreed to teach senior highs in the tower room or "belfry," as it was called in his church.

One day as he was getting ready to receive his truth seekers, a bat circled about him. And another. And another.

"Bats in the belfry!" he exclaimed. "I need a broom—I think."

And so it was that the man came down to the second story of the church building where he saw another teacher.

"Harry, there are bats in the belfry," he said. I need a—"

"You have to be joking," the other man said, turning his back and beginning to write on his chalkboard.

The teacher descended to the first floor, sought out the superintendent, and said, "Mrs. Cosgrove, there are bats in the —"

"Bats? *Bats?* BATS?" she shrieked and fainted.

This feat attracted the attention of the minister, because he was dashing due north to the sanctuary when the superintendent fell into his ribs, going south.

"Get a doctor!" he shouted, placing the limp and already conscious Mrs. Cosgrove on a bench in the hallway.

"She'll be all right," the man from the belfry assured his harried pastor. "I told her I had bats in the belfry, and she fainted at the mention of bats. I need a broom—I think. I've never battled bats before, but brooms—"

"See the custodian," said the pastor, heading north and leaving a fully recovered Mrs. Cosgrove on the bench.

In the basement, next to the furnace, the custodian had his office and his brooms. The man reported bats in the belfry.

"I'll tell you what," said the custodian, calm as water in a rain barrel. "You bring your class to my office, and I'll see what I can do with the bats."

"Oh, thank you, Sam. That's a great idea," the teacher told him.

"Nothing much, really," Sam answered. "If you want something done, find the fellow whose job it is to do it."

And that is the moral to this story.

CHAPTER 5

TWENTY QUESTIONS

Whom would you ask for help in answering the following questions? Which questions might you have to answer yourself?

1. Where may I watch someone teach students like mine?

2. Why did "they" think we could do what is suggested in this book?

3. Is my class dumb? This project isn't worth the sun power to dry it up.

4. I heard about those summer schools for church school teachers. How do I get to go to one?

5. Who can teach me to use a camcorder?

6. Those Lutherans on 81st Street are meeting every twenty-seven minutes with their teachers. Do you think Pastor Albrecht would let us come?

7. If I drive, who will go with me to Old Stone Church to learn what is new for middle schoolers?

8. I wish I knew who could get me in touch with a group of Jewish third- and fourth-graders. Who knows a rabbi or a Jewish teacher?

9. I asked the senior highs last week how many knew a Roman Catholic sister or priest. Not one did. Where can I meet one who would be good when exposed to my class. Could I get both a sister and a priest to teach for a few weeks?

10. I nearly had heart failure. Susie Payne had a seizure in class. Who can tell me what to do when that happens? She's so cute, so smart, and so likable that I

don't want her to feel she did something wrong.

11. My class wants to invite Woodlands out to do a puppet show with us. Is that all right? How do I approach them? I don't know anyone there personally.

12. I heard that Union Retirement Center likes to have singers come to their dining room. Do you know if they would enjoy our children's singing? We aren't a choir.

13. We made a video of three parables with Eldon McNabb's help. We would like to take it to another fourth-grade class. How do we connect with another church?

14. Our sixth-graders are studying the period between David and the exile. Is there a video that dramatizes the period?

15. I ordered that book from the address given in the periodical, and the letter came back. What can I do now?

16. That boy scares me. He stood for a whole hour with his finger tracing a jigsaw puzzle piece. His finger was bleeding. Surely, that isn't normal for a two-year-old.

17. Betsy Harris is pregnant and in ninth grade. She told me not to tell, but shouldn't I, in order to help her?

18. With five hundred dollars given us unexpectedly for kindergarten equipment, we want to know where to look for it, what to get, and where to order it. Who can help us?

19. I can't leave the city this summer. Is there any kind of teacher education I can take right here?

20. Do you think I should teach next year?

CHAPTER 6

A SONG TO REMEMBER

You can sing this song to the tune of "Pop Goes the Weasel" if you want to. Three important words are missing. You know what they are.

O, when you work with paper and paste
Or cones at Christmas season,
Don't forget to ask in your haste:
"What is the _____?"

Compose a song and put on a play,
There's really nothing to it,
Especially if nobody will say:
"_____ do we do it?"

Don't resign or quit in disgust.
Don't worry and be subjective.
You've neglected to note that all we do
Must have an _____.

CHAPTER 7

KEEP YOUR OWN LOG

Start collecting information and impressions you may cherish later and learn from too.

Collect whatever you think memorable, but collect. Humor was born of hindsight, and humor saves education from the pit. Collect funny anecdotes. Read them over often, especially those where the joke is on you. It has been purported that at least 20 percent of the Gospels show Jesus at his humorous best. Scholars with superb senses of humor themselves have disagreed, saying on the side that Jesus was not a standup comedian but that his audience, in its ignorance, was funny indeed. We are his audience. Some have caught on and laughed. Some have caught on and protested. Some cry. Some hope. Some pray.

And those who pray know that God is God no matter what we do or say as teachers in the house of God. Start your log right away.